The Imperfect Primary

Many people complain about the complex system used to nominate presidents. The system is hardly rational because it was never carefully planned. Because of the dissatisfaction over the idiosyncrasies of the current system, periodic calls arise to reform the presidential nomination process. But how are we to make sense of the myriad complexities in the system as well as in the calls for change?

In *The Imperfect Primary*, political scientist Barbara Norrander explores how presidential candidates are nominated, discusses past and current proposals for reform, and examines the possibility for more practical, incremental changes to the electoral rules. Norrander reminds us to be careful what we wish for—reforming the presidential nomination process is as complex as the current system. Through the modeling of empirical research to demonstrate how questions of biases can be systematically addressed, students can better see the advantages, disadvantages, and potential for unintended consequences in a whole host of reform proposals.

Barbara Norrander is a Professor in the School of Government and Public Policy at the University of Arizona. She has been writing about presidential nominations since the early 1980s.

Controversies in Electoral Democracy and Representation
Matthew J. Streb, Series Editor

The Routledge series *Controversies in Electoral Democracy and Representation* presents cutting edge scholarship and innovative thinking on a broad range of issues relating to democratic practice and theory. An electoral democracy, to be effective, must show a strong relationship between representation and a fair open election process. Designed to foster debate and challenge assumptions about how elections and democratic representation *should* work, titles in the series present a strong but fair argument on topics related to elections, voting behavior, party and media involvement, representation, and democratic theory.

The Imperfect Primary

Oddities, Biases, and Strengths of U.S. Presidential Nomination Politics

Barbara Norrander

Routledge
Taylor & Francis Group

NEW YORK AND LONDON

First published 2010
by Routledge
711 Third Avenue, New York, NY 10017

Simultaneously published in the UK
by Routledge
2 Park Square, Milton Park, Abingdon, Oxon OX14 4RN

*Routledge is an imprint of the Taylor & Francis Group,
an informa business*

© 2010 Taylor & Francis

Typeset in ITC Galliard by Glyph International Ltd.
Printed and bound in the United States of America on acid-free
paper by Edwards Brothers, Inc.

Library of Congress Cataloging in Publication Data
Norrander, Barbara, 1954–
The imperfect primary: oddities, biases, and strengths of U.S.
presidential nomination politics/Barbara Norrander.
      p.cm.
Includes bibliographical references and index.
1. Presidents–United States–Nomination.
2. Primaries–United States. I. Title.
JK522.N67 2010
324.273'154–dc22   2010005286

ISBN 13: 978-0-415-99545-0 (hbk)
ISBN 13: 978-0-415-99577-1 (pbk)
ISBN 13: 978-0-203-88767-7 (ebk)

Contents

4   Alternative Methods for Nominating Presidents

**5   Oddities, Biases, and Strengths of U.S. Presidential
Nomination Politics**

Figures

Tables

Preface

I came of voting age in 1972 just as primaries first came to dominate presidential nomination politics. In that year, George McGovern vied off against seven other Democrats to win convention delegates by winning primaries and caucuses. In 1976 Ronald Reagan almost unseated President Gerald Ford as the Republican nominee, while Jimmy Carter, an unknown former governor of Georgia, perfected momentum strategy. Presidential nomination politics settled down somewhat in the 1980s, but controversies still erupted over rules, strategies, and participants. No wonder I have been writing about presidential nomination politics ever since.

The 2008 presidential nominations once again brought a host of controversies to the forefront of public debate. The long battle between Senators Hillary Rodham Clinton and Barack Obama led to questions over the influence of superdelegates, whether the Democratic Party's use of proportional representation rules extended the nomination battle, and the role of caucuses. The Republican race more quickly came to a close, but the unfolding of the various candidates' strategies juxtaposed with their party's rules brought about this speedier conclusion. Many of the debates of 2008 echoed questions from previous election cycles, and these controversies have been addressed by existing political science research. For example, the effects of proportional representation versus winner-take-all rules were first investigated in connection with the 1972 nominations. The influence of superdelegates was initially explored for Walter Mondale's 1984 nomination. The uniqueness of the caucuses has been studied over the past 20 years for the nature of the participants and the differences in their outcomes. Thus, the 2008 nominations brought up many questions, but political scientists often already had many answers to offer.

My goal in writing this book was to address the oddities, biases, and strengths of the presidential nomination system in place at the beginning of the 21st century. Yet I wanted to do so from the perspective of the similarities with presidential nominations from the last quarter of the 20th century. This meant the first chapter of the book needed to cover the ever-changing presidential nomination process from the early 19th century to the beginning of the 21st century. Rather than focusing solely on the 2008 nomination battles in Chapter 2, my aim was to show the recurring patterns in the 2000–2008 quests for both parties' presidential slots. Chapter 3 investigates biases in voting rules, caucuses, delegate allocation and distribution, superdelegates, and the front-loaded nomination calendar. This chapter, in particular, was informed by the existing research in political science. The numerous reform proposals became the topic for Chapter 4. The book closes out with a reminder of how oddities, biases, and strengths are found in a number of electoral settings as well as in presidential nomination politics.

For students reading this book, I hope to make them better consumers of the depictions of the politics of recent and future presidential nominations. To do so, I want to give students a bit of historical perspective. I also wish to introduce students to a bit of empirical research to demonstrate how questions of biases can be scientifically addressed. New reforms for presidential nomination procedures are frequently debated, and I want students to be able to see the advantages, disadvantages, and potential for unintended consequences in such proposals. Finally, I want to leave students with the message that electoral politics is an area of unique events unfolding within structures that provide both continuity and change in procedures and outcomes.

This book would not have come about without the urging of Matthew J. Streb, series editor for Routledge's Controversies in Electoral Democracy and Representation. Matt Streb and Michael Kerns, acquisitions editor for Routledge, convinced me that a book about the peculiarities of presidential nomination politics needed to be written. Lonna Atkeson of the University of New Mexico, Audrey Haynes of the University of Georgia, and Richard Pious of Barnard College reviewed the original book proposal and made helpful suggestions for improving the project. Several colleagues provided useful comments on the completed manuscript. Lonna Atkeson and Clyde Wilcox shared their informed perspectives on the topic of each chapter. Carol Norrander used her insight as a middle school teacher to help with the readability of the manuscript. Of course, any remaining errors or confusion are solely my responsibility. I also wish to thank Sylvia Manzano for offering to prepare the maps used in Chapter 4. Finally, the book would not have come to fruition without the careful work of the production staff at Routledge, in particular Mary Altman, Siân Findlay, Felicity Watts, and Sophie Cox.

Chapter 1

Happenstance and Reforms

In July 2007, John McCain's campaign coffers were nearly empty. McCain's second try for the Republican presidential nomination was not going as planned. After spending $24 million in early 2007 trying to project an air of inevitability for winning the nomination, McCain's fundraising had been less than expected and he had fallen behind former New York mayor Rudy Giuliani in the national public opinion polls by 15 percentage points.[1] Though McCain had strong foreign policy credentials, some factions of the Republican Party continued to distrust McCain due to his positions on immigration and campaign finance reform. To restart his campaign, McCain fired most of his staff and went back to the tactic that had seemed to work in 2000. He got on a bus and began his cross-country "No Surrender Tour." McCain emphasized his support for a surge of troops in the Iraq War and gradually the crowds at his rallies began to increase.

McCain also bet that none of his competitors would be able to unite the Republican Party. While Giuliani led in the opinion polls, his positions on social issues would be too liberal for many traditional Republicans. Mitt Romney, the former governor of Massachusetts, had raised the most campaign funds, and as a successful business leader he had strong credentials for economic policies. Yet, Romney was often wooden on the campaign trail, and he was accused of flip-flopping on social issues because he had switched to a more conservative position on abortion. Former Arkansas governor Mike Huckabee was consolidating the party's religious conservatives behind him, but would he be able to expand beyond this base to incorporate the party's economic and foreign policy conservatives? Fred Thompson might have a chance to unite these factions, but he appeared to be a reluctant campaigner.

On the Democratic side in July 2007, New York senator Hillary Rodham Clinton was clearly in command. She had secured the support of many of the party's elite, she raised large sums of money, and the media and her opponents treated her as the frontrunner. Other senior senators, such as Chris Dodd and Joe Biden, were unable to keep up in fundraising totals or in the national polls. John Edwards, in his second try for the presidential nomination, also lagged behind Clinton. Each of these candidates would need an early primary or caucus victory or a major mistake by Clinton to have a realistic chance at winning the nomination. Illinois senator Barack Obama had been on the national stage for only four years, being introduced to the national audience with his keynote address at the 2004 Democratic convention and being elected to the U.S. Senate in 2006. Could he compete with Clinton? Obama was almost as successful as Clinton in raising campaign funds and his rallies drew large crowds, but he was awkward in the early debates, some of the party's elite were wary of supporting such an untested candidate, and the general public too seemed unimpressed as Obama trailed Clinton in the national polls by 20 percentage points.[2]

Results from the early caucuses and primaries would set the tone for both parties' 2008 nomination contests. On the Republican side, Huckabee won the opening round in Iowa, with the support of the large number of religious conservatives in the Iowa Republican Party. Romney finished a disappointing second, given the amount of money he spent campaigning in Iowa. McCain won in New Hampshire, as he had done in 2000. This time, McCain was able to follow up with crucial victories in the South Carolina and Florida primaries. McCain was now the frontrunner. Next came February 5, Super Duper Tuesday, when nearly half of the states would hold their primaries or caucuses. McCain won two-thirds of the Super Duper Tuesday primaries and became the Republican Party's presumptive nominee.

In March 2008, McCain accumulated the final number of convention delegates, half of the total, necessary to be guaranteed the Republican Party's presidential nomination. McCain earned the support of these delegates by winning 33 of the 41 Republican primary elections and 6 of the 17 caucuses. (The number of primaries and caucuses adds up to more than 50 because a few states held both a primary and a caucus, plus Washington, DC, Puerto Rico, and U.S. territories, such as Guam, also participate with caucuses or primaries.) More importantly, as McCain increasingly won more of the presidential primaries throughout January and early February, one-by-one his competitors for the nomination dropped out of the race. Fred Thompson and Rudy Giuliani left in January. Mitt Romney exited the contest after Super Duper Tuesday. When McCain accumulated the last of the delegates needed for the nomination in the first week of March, his last serious challenger, Mike Huckabee, also withdrew from the race.

The only remaining question was who would be McCain's running mate, and he announced his choice of Alaska governor Sarah Palin on August 29, three days before the Republican Party convention would open in St. Paul, Minnesota. The goal of the Republican convention was to rally the party behind its presidential ticket. Palin galvanized the party's base with her convention speech emphasizing her background as a small town mayor and a hockey mom while attacking the Democratic ticket and the Washington establishment. On the final day of the Republican convention, McCain gave his acceptance speech before 2,380 Republican delegates and a national and international television, radio, and internet audience. In his speech, McCain promised he would fight for the rights, prosperity, and security of America.

The 2008 Democratic nomination opened with an unexpected upset of Clinton in the Iowa caucuses. Obama more successfully mobilized his supporters to turn out for these two-hour Thursday night meetings. Clinton came back with a dramatic win in New Hampshire. The two candidates split the next two contests in Nevada and South Carolina. On Super Duper Tuesday, Clinton and Obama again split the states. Clinton originally planned to secure the nomination with victories on Super Duper Tuesday and did not have a strategy for a long campaign. Obama knew he needed to gather every possible delegate if he was going to upset Clinton, and his delegate totals inched above Clinton's with victories in caucuses and primaries held later in February. Yet, Clinton came back with important victories in states such as Ohio and Pennsylvania. The Democratic nomination battle continued until the last two primaries held on June 3, when Obama secured the necessary delegate total for winning the Democratic nomination. Senator Clinton conceded the nomination to Senator Obama at a speech before her supporters on June 7.

Many speculated whether the bitter battle between Obama and Clinton would harm the party's fortunes in the fall election. Yet, Senator Clinton and former president Bill Clinton both endorsed Obama, helped with his campaign during the summer, and gave hearty endorsement speeches at the Democratic convention. At the convention, the roll call of states, which announces the delegate support for each candidate, was orchestrated to halt at New York, where Senator Clinton asked the convention to nominate Obama by acclamation. A quick voice vote approved the motion. The following evening, in a session moved to Denver's professional football stadium, Obama's acceptance speech echoed the themes of his primary campaign: "Change We Can Believe In."

Modern presidential nominations are secured by winning the support of the American electorate in primaries and caucuses. But the process is twofold. At one level it is a national contest between the competing candidates. Every candidate wants to win as many primaries as possible, and in particular, wants to win in the early primaries and caucuses. Doing well in these early events gives a candidate the reputation and resources to compete in subsequent primaries. Doing poorly in the early primaries often leads candidates to withdraw from the contest. In most cases in recent years, all but one candidate has withdrawn from the nomination contest before all of the primaries are held. This one remaining candidate becomes the party's presumptive nominee.

The second level of the twofold process is the legal component. In two-thirds of the states the public's vote in a presidential primary is linked to the selection of delegates who will represent the state at the party's national convention. In the remaining states, the public participates in neighborhood caucuses, which are open party meetings, where they select some attendees to be delegates to higher level conventions and eventually the national convention. It is the votes of these delegates at the two parties' national conventions that officially name the nominees. While technically selected from each state, today these delegates are strongly committed, and in some instances legally bound, to support a particular candidate. Thus, the convention vote can be predicted beforehand by counting up the delegates committed to each candidate. A candidate who controls the support of 50 percent of the convention delegates will become the party's nominee.

The pathways to the 2008 presidential nominations were complex and chaotic. Nearly half the states chose a single day in February for their primary or caucus. A few states were allowed to go earlier and the rest were relegated to the end of the line. This scheduling of states' primaries across different dates made some events more important than others. Take the Pennsylvania primary, for example. This event held on April 22 was a crucial battle between Barack Obama and Hillary Clinton. Both campaigned heavily in the state: Obama spent $10 million on television advertisements while Clinton's spending totaled to $5 million.[3] More than two million registered Pennsylvania Democrats voted in their primary for a turnout rate of approximately 60 percent. Yet for Republicans in Pennsylvania, their party's primary was anticlimactic. John McCain had already secured the number of delegates needed to win the Republican nomination, and all of the other major contenders had bowed out of the race. Only 800,000 Republicans, or one in four, bothered to vote in the Republican primary. Pennsylvania Democrats sure appeared to have more influence on their party's choice for the presidential nomination than did Pennsylvania Republicans.

The rules for winning convention delegates varied across states and the two parties. In the February 5 New Jersey Democratic primary, Hillary Clinton won the support of 54 percent of the voters. Under Democratic Party proportional representation rules, she was allocated 59 of the 107 delegates from the state. On the Republican side of the ballot in New Jersey, John McCain won 55 percent of the vote but was awarded all of the Republican delegates. Some Republican convention delegates are awarded under such winner-take-all rules, others by proportional representation. Some Republican delegates are directly elected, and in some caucuses, there are no formal rules at all. Commentators often argue that the Democratic Party's proportional representation rules needlessly prolonged the battle between Obama and Clinton. Others feel that the awarding of all of a state's delegates to one candidate discounts the voices of the voters who supported other candidates.

The number of delegates a candidate could win in a single state also varied across the two parties. The vote from New York's Democratic primary would allocate 232 convention delegates, or 6.8 percent of the total of pledged delegates. The New York Republican primary was allotted 98 delegates, or 4.4 percent of the potential pledged total.[4] In this case, it appears that New York Democrats have more influence on their party's nomination than do New York Republicans. Yet, New York is often a state in the Democratic column for presidential elections, and so its Democratic primary voters might warrant a greater say.

How Americans participate in the nomination process also varies across the states. Participation in primaries may be restricted to those who are registered with the party or it may be open to all voters. To participate in a caucus an individual needs to attend a local party meeting at a specific time and place. Those with work, school, or family commitments at this time cannot participate. The number of people willing and able to participate in a caucus may be extremely small. On the other hand, those who do attend the caucuses participate in a setting where they debate with their neighbors the merits of the various candidates. Such discrepancies between the two parties and across the states often lead to renewed calls for more reforms of the presidential nomination process.

The procedures used to nominate candidates for America's highest office have evolved over the years. Sometimes, the process changed due to deliberate plans of the parties or a group of reformers. At other times, changes happened more by happenstance. For example, the front-loaded primary calendar, where in 2008 nearly half the states held their primaries or caucuses on February 5, was not a planned event. Rather individual states wanted more clout, and all took the same path of moving their primary dates forward. The current nomination process is a hodgepodge of past reform movements, rules instituted by national and state parties, strategic behaviors of candidates, the actions of campaign professionals and campaign contributors, the involvement of citizen activists, and a few state and national laws. No grand scheme was used to create a rational system to nominate the candidates for the nation's chief executive office. The process is one that is constantly evolving: sometimes by leaps, sometimes by inches. The procedures are complicated, and the outcome subject to chance events.

Calls for reforming the presidential nomination system are now nearly 100 years old. In 1911, the first bill was introduced into Congress to establish a one-day national primary. In more recent years, congressional bills and other reform proposals have centered on clustering primaries on specific dates by geographic region or state population sizes. None of the more than 300 bills introduced into Congress has been enacted into law.[5] Yet, a demand for reform remains. In the early months of 2008, a number of newspaper editorials advocated for restructuring the process. The Portland *Oregonian* editorial, under the headline "A Helter-Skelter Primary System," lent its support to the regional primary format. The *Boston Globe* editorial, "Primary Train Wreck," asserted that "Reform is overdue." The *New York Times, Columbus Dispatch, Santa Fe New Mexican, Kansas City Star, Sacramento Bee*, and a host of other newspapers called for a switch to a regional or population-based primary schedule.[6] The current system was viewed as too muddled and too biased. Yet, a few voices were heard in support of the current process. *Newsweek* columnist George F. Will argued that while the process is messy it produces the desired results. The public learns about the candidates through the staggered primary process, which allows them to make a meaningful choice among the candidates seeking the two parties' presidential nominations. Further, Will argues that this choice occurs within a framework of federalism that gives individual states wide discretion in their selection of rules and formats for public participation.[7]

The goal of this book is to make the reader a wiser consumer of such claims for and against reforming the presidential nomination system. To do so, the first chapter will explain how we got to today. What were the reforms and changes that led to a presidential nominating system at the beginning of the 21st century that was dominated by primary elections, many of which were sandwiched together on one early date in the election calendar? The second chapter concentrates on the 2000, 2004, and 2008 nominations for the Democratic and Republican parties. How did candidates' assets, public opinion, primary outcomes, and candidate attrition contribute to the outcomes of these presidential nominations? In Chapter 3, the messiness and potential biases of the current nomination process are analyzed. What are the effects of rules concerning delegate selection, citizen participation, and the election calendar? Chapter 4 looks at the various reforms and discusses the pros and cons of each. The final chapter reviews the oddities, biases, and strengths of the U.S. presidential nomination process.

A Short History of Presidential Nominations

The nomination of Abraham Lincoln by the Republican Party in 1860 was vastly different from the paths to the nomination taken by John McCain or Barack Obama in 2008. In May 1860, Republicans met in Chicago to name their presidential nominee. No one knew in advance who this nominee would be. Primary elections did not exist, nor did reliable public opinion polls. If there was a frontrunner for the nomination, it was

New York senator William Henry Seward. An outspoken opponent of slavery, Seward had the backing of powerful eastern financial interests and numerous loyal supporters who came to Chicago to advocate for his candidacy. The New York delegation alone, comprised of 70 individuals, would provide one-third of the needed 233 votes. Seward, however, was opposed by the southern state delegations, and he had limited support from the western states.[8]

A variety of other politicians were contenders for the Republican nomination, as well. Ohio senator Salmon Portland Chase was a vocal opponent of slavery, and as such, a competitor to Seward for the same faction of the party. Chase would have to overcome his past affiliations with the Democratic Party and his opposition to the tariff, a tax on imports, supported by the manufacturing interests. Although Edward Bates from Missouri also opposed slavery, being from a border state might make him more acceptable to southerners. On the other hand, Bates had offended recent immigrants with his previous support of the Know-Nothings movement, with its anti-immigrant, anti-Catholic, anti-slavery, and pro-temperance positions. Another possibility was Supreme Court Justice John McLean, but he was 73 years old, in ill health, and needed as an anti-slavery vote on the high court. The Pennsylvania delegation would support its favorite son, Senator Simon Cameron.

The Illinois delegation also had a favorite-son candidate: Abraham Lincoln, a former one-term congressman known for oratorical skills. Two years earlier, Lincoln had faced Democrat Stephen Douglas in a series of seven debates as each sought the Illinois seat in the U.S. Senate. Senators at the time were appointed by the state legislatures, so the debates were aimed at the members of the Illinois state legislature. Still, these debates received widespread newspaper coverage. The topic was slavery and its expansion into the western territories and new states. Douglas advocated letting residents of the new states decide, while Lincoln opposed any expansion of slavery. The state legislature selected Douglas over Lincoln. Prior to the 1860 convention, Lincoln's speeches were reissued in a series of books. Yet, Lincoln remained an unknown in the East. Although at the time it was deemed unseemly to campaign for the presidential nomination, Lincoln in the year before the convention engaged in a series of 23 speeches to Republican gatherings across the nation to increase his reputation.

At the convention, each candidate's handlers maneuvered to put together a winning coalition. Behind the scenes, Lincoln's handlers negotiated with several states to consolidate the anti-Seward vote. If Lincoln could deny Seward the needed votes on the first ballot, he could pick up the support of additional states on the second. Lincoln's handlers also packed the spectator seats with Lincoln supporters, some with counterfeit tickets which denied seats to Seward's backers. Seward led on the first two ballots but could not gain the majority of the votes needed. On the third ballot, Lincoln pulled ahead and won the nomination. Lincoln never attended the convention. As was the custom of the time, he waited at his home in Springfield for a delegation from the convention to come tell him of the nomination. Along with nominating Lincoln, the 1860 Republican convention ratified its platform opposing the expansion of slavery, supporting a tariff to protect American industry, and proposing a homestead act to provide land to western settlers.

The 1860 Republican convention was vastly different from those held in 2008. First and foremost, in the 1800s the identity of the party's nominee was not known prior to the convention. Each candidate's handlers bargained with the state delegations, some of which were controlled by party bosses, to gain support for their candidate. Deals were struck in smoke-filled back rooms between a candidate's handlers and various state leaders. But events on the convention floor also could galvanize the delegates, such as in 1896 when William Jennings Bryan's "Cross of Gold" speech against the tight money standards of the day led to his nomination, despite his youth and lack of a national reputation. Party leaders in the 1800s had three goals in mind when selecting a candidate. They wanted a candidate who could unify the party, who represented the party's positions on the issues of the day, and most importantly, who could win the fall election. These three goals are shared by the parties today, but the primaries and caucuses provide the information on the issue positions and electoral strength of the candidates. The major role of the convention has become to ensure party unity.

Two Early Views: Nomination by Political Elites

The Founders' Plan?

The U.S. Constitution does not cover how candidates would be nominated for the presidency or any other office. Most aspects of elections, such as voter eligibility, would be left up to the states. In addition, the Constitution contains no mention of political parties. At the Constitutional Convention, the founders struggled with devising a method for selecting the country's chief executive, not the nomination of candidates to be considered for that selection. Various plans were debated before settling on an Electoral College made up of temporary electors who would cast ballots from the states to choose the president. The method of selecting these electors would be left up to the states, whether they were appointed by the state legislatures or elected by the public. The founders' reasons for settling on the Electoral College were varied. Some harbored a distrust of the average citizen's ability to select a chief executive, and it was a common practice at the time to have indirect selection for government offices. The electors, presumably, would be the political and economic elite of a state who would conscientiously consider the merits of various candidates. Smaller states favored an indirect method because they feared that a directly elected president would always come from the more populous states. Others made a theoretical argument that the Electoral College would allow for an independent executive branch, rather than one appointed by the legislature, as was common in the state governments of the day. Finally, a temporary Electoral College was viewed as less susceptible to corruption than the national legislature.[9]

While the founders did not create a mechanism for nominating candidates, without political parties to structure the vote in the Electoral College, it would function more as a nominating board than as a body to select the president.[10] Each state's Electoral College members would meet on the same day but in their own state capital. Given the hardships of communications, these electors would be operating independently from one another. As a result, Electoral College votes would be scattered among national, regional, and even state leaders. No one candidate would have sufficient support to meet the 50 percent requirement needed to win. Instead, Congress would choose the president from among the top contenders. George Mason, commenting at the Constitutional Convention, noted that this was the expected pattern 19 out of 20 times: the Electoral College would nominate, and Congress would elect the president.

Coordination of preferences across the states, however, would make the Electoral College a decisive mechanism for electing presidents. In the first presidential election, Alexander Hamilton worked behind the scenes to ensure that the electors supported the team of George Washington for president and John Adams for vice president.[11] During the Washington administration, political parties developed inside of Congress. The Federalist Party was led by Alexander Hamilton and supported policies for a stronger national government. The Democratic-Republican Party favored state governments and formed around Thomas Jefferson. When George Washington announced that he would not seek a third term in 1796, the two parties turned to the meetings of their members in Congress, i.e., the congressional caucuses, to select the party's nominee for the presidency.[12] With the parties coordinating the Electoral College vote around two competing candidates, one candidate was likely to garner 50 percent of the Electoral College votes and win the presidential election.

Congressional Caucus: 1800–1824

The congressional caucuses nominated the presidential candidates for a period of 20 years. In the beginning, these congressional caucuses had many merits. They provided an authoritative nomination for each party. Given the difficulty of travel and communications in the early

19th century, the congressional caucuses provided a ready-made meeting of party leaders. The presidency was a national office, and the national parties controlled the nominations. In fact, a norm developed for prominent politicians to first hold the office of Secretary of State and then become the party's presidential nominee.

By 1820 the Federalist Party had lost much of its strength and did not nominate a candidate for president. The country had only one remaining national party, the Democratic-Republican Party. By 1824 a number of party leaders wanted the presidential bid. William Crawford was nominated by the congressional caucus, but this process was becoming increasingly discredited. Many party members did not participate in the caucus in 1824, and it earned the nickname of "King Caucus." Three other candidates ran as presidential candidates from the Democratic-Republican Party in 1824, being nominated by various state legislatures. With a four-person contest, no candidate won a majority in the Electoral College. Congress selected John Quincy Adams to be president, though Andrew Jackson had the largest percent of the original Electoral College vote.

What had happened to the reputation of the congressional caucus? Mostly, the political landscape changed quickly in the first 20 years of the 19th century. Most states switched from limiting the electorate to wealthy or propertied men to allowing all white males to vote. The selection of members of the Electoral College moved from the state legislatures to a public vote. The development of a partisan press allowed for a wider, national debate over government policies. The political parties were no longer merely groups of men in Congress, but now they were organizations of leaders and voters in state and local politics. These newer party members wanted a say in the presidential nominations. Thus, the congressional caucuses came to be viewed as unrepresentative and undemocratic. The system also lacked a true separation of powers between the executive and legislative branches, because Congress was nominating the presidential candidates.[13]

In 1828, Andrew Jackson won the presidency and transformed the Democratic-Republican Party into the Democratic Party, though the name change did not officially occur until 1844. This new party favored patronage to fill government positions, rewarding political supporters with government posts. Jackson's Democratic Party also opposed the nationalistic policies of the old Federalist Party, preferring power to be held by the states rather than the national government. States would be allowed to run their own governments and economies, including economies based on slavery. The opposition would eventually form into the Whig Party. Democrats versus Whigs became the second party system in U.S. history. This new mass-based party system needed a more democratic means to nominate the president.

The Party Convention Eras

Autonomous Conventions: 1832–1908

The answer to the new, authoritative nominating system was the national convention. These conventions would bring together representatives of the party from all the states, but these convention delegates would be short-term representatives. Once the business of nominating the president was completed, the conventions would disband. Following the example of the small Anti-Masonic Party, the Democratic Party held its first national convention in Baltimore in 1832. The Whigs adopted the practice in 1839.

The convention system transferred party power from the national legislature to the state parties. States were given leeway in the method for selecting their convention delegates. In some states, the governor or a state-level party committee would appoint the delegates. More frequently, local party meetings, also called caucuses, would select delegates to attend county caucuses, then a state convention, and finally the national convention. The delegates represented the state parties, not a preference for a political candidate. State parties might even choose to impose a unit rule, requiring all of their delegates to vote as a whole. The Republican Party never adopted the unit rule, but the Democratic Party did not formally ban the unit rule until 1968 by which time only four states still used it. The Democratic Party until 1936 also required a presidential candidate to win the support of two-thirds of all delegates to become the nominee. This rule was to protect the smaller states from being consistently overpowered by the larger states. It also provided the southern states with a veto over any Democratic nominee.[14]

Nomination politics in this classic era of political conventions often meant that multiple ballots were needed before one candidate emerged as a winner. These roll calls of state delegations were the indicators of support for the various candidates. If a candidate's support failed to grow between roll calls, he could be forced out of the contest. If a candidate increased his support from one roll call to the next, other delegates would look more favorably on him. In fact, state delegations wanted to join the group of delegates supporting a candidate just before he would secure enough votes to win the nomination; they could then make greater claims on the candidate if he won the election. This process of strategically moving toward a winning candidate was called jumping on the candidate's bandwagon. Some states held off their support in the early rounds by supporting a home-state candidate, called a favorite son, rather than casting their ballots for one of the national contenders. Other states were controlled by a party boss who could bargain with the candidates' operatives to throw the weight of his state behind one of the national contenders.

In some conventions, a stalemate occurred between two leading contenders, neither of whom could secure the required number of votes needed for the nomination. In these cases, the convention might turn to a new compromise candidate, who was called a dark horse, since he had little chance of winning the nomination in the initial rounds. In 1844, James K. Polk became the first dark-horse candidate to win a presidential nomination when he secured the needed votes on the 9th ballot.

The political conventions of the mid- to late 19th century were autonomous bodies. They determined who would become the presidential nominees through internal bargaining. They had to because no other mechanisms existed to judge the support of the candidates: no public opinion polls, no primary elections. In addition, the norm against candidates engaging in preconvention campaigning also gave few clues as to the strengths and weaknesses of potential nominees. Thus, the convention delegates battled it out over the nominees. They also, after 1840, developed a list of party issues, called a platform. At times, the battle over the nomination became intertwined with battles over the platform, as when William Jennings Bryan's speech in the platform debate over the gold standard led to his nomination.

Mostly Autonomous Conventions: 1912–1944

The legal process for nominating presidential candidates remained the same in the first half of the 20th century. Indeed, the legal process of being named by the party's national convention is still in place today. What changed was the ability of the convention to name a candidate independent of outside influences. During the first half of the 20th century presidential primaries were introduced and reliable public opinion polling methods were devised. Both could provide information on the popular appeal of the various candidates. Candidates also altered their behavior, engaging in more overt preconvention campaigning. The nature of the conventions also changed, with fewer state party bosses and more avenues for national interest groups to play a role. Finally, the conventions became more public, with radio coverage beginning in 1924. Television coverage would arrive in 1948.

With more public information on candidate strengths and weaknesses, with fewer traditional bargaining agents within the convention, and with the constraints of doing business under the glare of a national audience, protracted fights over the nomination, involving multiple roll calls, gradually disappeared. A few conventions reverted back to the old style, with the 1924 Democratic convention using 103 ballots (the most ever) over a three-week period before settling on the nomination of John W. Davis. The Republicans used 10 ballots in 1920 to nominate Warren Harding. Since those instances, the only multiple ballot nominations on the Democratic side have been four ballots to nominate Franklin Delano Roosevelt in 1932 and three to nominate Adlai Stevenson in 1952. The Republicans used six ballots to nominate Wendell Willkie in 1940 and three in 1948 to put forward Thomas Dewey's name as their nominee. Yet, more and more nominations were being decided on the first ballot, going to a predetermined national favorite.

Conventions in the early 20th century also began to center more on the candidates, with candidates now coming to the convention. In 1932 Franklin Delano Roosevelt was the first major party candidate to give an acceptance speech at the convention. In 1944, the Republican Party joined in when Thomas E. Dewey gave an acceptance speech. Presidential nominee acceptance speeches are now the final activity of conventions and planned for primetime media coverage.

The Origins of Presidential Primaries

During the first two decades of the 20th century, states adopted primary laws to select party candidates for local and state offices, as well as for members of Congress. These primaries were part of the Progressive Movement's series of reforms to bring more political power to the public and away from the parties, which many viewed as corrupt. In these direct primaries, the candidate who won the most votes (e.g., a plurality voting rule) automatically became the party's nominee. Southern states developed their own tradition of requiring an absolute majority of the vote for nomination, which led to runoff primaries when no candidate won 50 percent of the vote in the initial round.

While almost all states adopted the direct primary to nominate representatives or governors, far fewer adopted presidential primaries. Further, presidential primaries would be an indirect voice for the public. Presidential primaries would select convention delegates, who would continue to choose the presidential nominees. Florida in 1904 became the first state to select its convention delegates through a primary. Voters in Florida's presidential primary cast ballots directly for individual convention delegates, but at no place on the ballot were the presidential candidate preferences of these potential delegates listed. A 1906 Pennsylvania law allowed delegates to list their preferred presidential candidate, but none of those competing to be delegates in the 1908 Democratic or Republican primaries did so. The first separate preference vote for presidential candidates came in Oregon in 1912, in a law that also required all delegates elected to support the candidate that won the preference primary.[15]

Advocates argued primaries would reduce political corruption, reduce the influence of party bosses at the state and national levels, give rank-and-file supporters a voice in nominations, and educate voters about the merits of the various candidates.[16] Opponents of the primary process averred primaries would not lead to the selection of a candidate who could win the general election as well as small, face-to-face groups at the convention could. Further, primaries could be divisive—supporters of losing candidates would be unwilling to vote for the winning candidate in the fall election. Primaries would not cure corruption, they argued, because it would take money to win. Finally, they asserted that few voters would participate.[17]

The first extensive use of presidential primaries occurred in 1912. Former president Theodore Roosevelt decided to once again seek the presidency. He entered 12 of the 13 primaries, winning 9 of them. The Republican convention, however, renominated sitting president William Howard Taft instead. Angered by his defeat at the convention, Roosevelt ran as a third-party candidate under the Progressive or Bull Moose label. With two Republican candidates (Roosevelt, Taft) and only one Democratic candidate (Woodrow Wilson) running in the 1912 presidential election, the Democratic candidate won despite the fact that the Republican Party was the larger party at the time. Thus, the first real test of presidential primaries proved one of the criticisms of the opponents: primaries could be divisive.

The number of states using presidential primaries rose to 26 in 1916, but with World War I the Progressive reform era came to an end. Presidential primaries fell into disfavor. Many party leaders viewed them as too costly for candidates, the parties, and state governments. The 1930s brought the New Deal realignment, with greater interparty differences between the Democratic and Republican parties. Policy conflicts were focused between the two parties rather than within either party. This too led to fewer calls for party reform. Over time, states rescinded presidential primary laws, resulting in 16 or 17 states holding primaries during any election year through the 1960s.[18]

Even the presidential primaries that remained in place were not an important part of the nomination process. The Democratic Party had few nomination decisions to make in the 1930s and 1940s as they renominated President Franklin Delano Roosevelt three times. Candidates seeing that fewer than half of the convention delegates were selected in primaries, and that winning primaries did not necessarily mean winning the nomination, did not campaign in them. Primary ballots, rather than containing the names of national candidates, listed favorite-son candidates or unpledged delegates. Thus, after 1912, primaries did not play a role in presidential nominations during the first half of the 20th century.

Public influence on nominations in the early to mid-20th century came mainly through public opinion surveys rather than voting at the polls. The party elite wanted to nominate a popular candidate for the top of the ticket with the assumption that voters who cast a ballot for the party's presidential candidate would continue to vote for the party's candidates for other offices further down the ballot. The beginning of scientific public opinion polling in the 1930s provided a reliable indicator of public preferences. From 1936 to 1972 the candidate who led in the Gallup poll prior to the primaries won the nomination 85 percent of the time. During this time period, the results of the primaries also had little influence in changing these national preferences: 90 percent of the time the pre-primary poll leader remained the poll leader after the primaries were over.[19]

A Mixed System: Conventions and Primaries, 1948–1960

After World War II, presidential primaries became a somewhat more important component of the presidential nomination process, but they still would not be the dominant way for a candidate to win the nomination or the most typical method for selecting convention delegates. The major change came in candidates' strategies. Increasingly some candidates began to view presidential primaries as a component of their strategy—not to win the nomination outright but to prove to party leaders that they could win votes. Thus, the nomination process during this period is best viewed as a mixed system: partly a primary strategy but partly a semi-autonomous convention.

A change in candidate strategy after World War II helped to revitalize the presidential primaries with some candidates actively campaigning in the primary states in order to win victories. This new candidate strategy was possibly due to changes in air travel, allowing candidates to campaign in primaries scattered across the nation, and a more nationalized media (e.g., radio followed by television) which would bring the results of these primaries to a national audience. Yet, many of the candidates who tried the new primary-centered campaign tactic failed to win the presidential nomination. Party leaders at the conventions still had the decisive voice in the nomination, and too few delegates were chosen through the primary process to gain control of a majority of the delegates. Presidential primary victories were one tool that candidates could employ, but it was a risky tool. Primary victories could help a candidate's reputation, but a primary loss often signaled the end of a campaign. Thus, not all candidates pursued the primary route as part of their campaign strategy.

John F. Kennedy's 1960 nomination strategy shows the mixed mode method of seeking the presidential nomination during this era.[20] After losing his bid to be the Democratic Party's vice presidential nominee in 1956, Kennedy set out to court party leaders across the country. He made numerous visits to state and local party events, building a personal connection to the far flung party members who were the core of the party activists at the time. Yet, Kennedy still needed to demonstrate to these leaders that he could win votes. So he entered 7 of the 16 primaries held in 1960. Two proved to be the most important. The first was the Wisconsin primary, where his defeat over Minnesota senator Hubert Humphrey demonstrated Kennedy's greater popular appeal in Humphrey's own region of the country. Kennedy's West Virginia primary victory was important to prove that a Catholic candidate could win in a heavily Protestant state. With the personal connections Kennedy made with his cross-country trips and his victories in select primaries, Kennedy secured the 1960 Democratic nomination. Not all candidates in that year pursued the nomination by entering the primaries, as Kennedy and Humphrey had. Texas senator Lyndon Johnson, who was also the majority party leader in the Senate, calculated that Kennedy and Humphrey would knock each other out of the race with a mixed record of primary wins and losses. The regular party members at the national convention, Johnson reasoned, would then turn to him to be the nominee.

By the time of the mixed system of primaries and conventions, the conventions had lost much of their autonomy. The conventions were now constrained by primary results, if one candidate was successful, and by other indicators of candidate popularity, such as public opinion polls. The conventions were public affairs, unfolding before a national television audience. In an often quoted assessment, William Carleton in 1957 asserted that

> It is probable that by 1976 or 1980 all that a nominating convention will do will be to meet to ratify the nomination for president of *the* national favorite already determined by *the* agencies, formal and informal, of mass democracy; . . . to endorse a platform already written by leaders responding to national and group pressures; and to stage a rally for the benefit of the national television audience. Delegates and "leaders" in national conventions, like presidential electors, will have become rubber stamps. [21]

Carleton's predictions came to fruition in the 1970s after a series of party reforms and individual state actions developed a new nominating system that was dominated by the presidential primaries.

Moving to a Primary-Dominated System

Initial movements toward reforms in the Democratic Party began in the 1950s, but came to a head at the 1968 convention. The early movement toward national standards for delegate selection to Democratic conventions centered on divisions in the party over civil rights. After the Democratic Party adopted a civil rights platform at its 1948 convention, some southern delegates walked out. In the fall election, Strom Thurmond ran for president as a Dixiecrat (formally called the States' Rights Democratic Party), replacing the national Democratic ticket in four states.

Northern Democrats responded with a demand for party loyalty from future convention delegates, and the 1956 convention rules required state delegations to assure placement of the Democratic ticket on their state's ballot.

In 1964, two competing groups of delegates were chosen from Mississippi, the regular Democratic Party delegation containing only whites and the Mississippi Freedom Democratic Party delegation containing mostly blacks. After a lengthy Credentials Committee debate, the convention adopted a compromise of seating the regular Mississippi delegation but requiring them to pledge to support the national Democratic ticket, seating two of the Freedom Party leaders as delegates, and requiring that for the 1968 convention no state delegation would be seated that limited participation by race.

The compromise was not universally accepted: the Mississippi and Alabama delegations walked out and the Freedom Party supporters protested. Nevertheless, the 1964 Democratic convention established the Special Equal Rights Committee which created six delegate selection guidelines for the 1968 convention that would prohibit racial discrimination in each state's method of selecting delegates. At the 1968 convention, the Credentials Committee did deny seats to the regular Mississippi delegation and replaced it with the Loyal Democrat delegation chosen under nondiscriminatory rules. Thus, by the early 1960s, the national Democratic Party had begun to make rules on who could be delegates and how they would be selected. [22]

In 1968, the Democratic Party was deeply divided over the Vietnam War. Minnesota senator Eugene McCarthy decided to challenge President Lyndon Johnson's renomination. College students cut their hair, getting "Clean for Gene," to campaign for the anti-war candidate in the New Hampshire primary scheduled for March 12. In that Democratic primary, McCarthy's total of 42.4 percent to Johnson's 49.5 percent was enough for the media to call McCarthy the "winner." On March 16, New York senator Robert Kennedy entered the race as the second anti-war candidate. On March 31, President Johnson abruptly left the race for the Democratic nomination asserting he could not negotiate an end to the war at the same time as he was running for reelection. Vice President Hubert Humphrey was encouraged by party leaders to step into the race as Johnson's replacement. He did, but Humphrey did not run in the remaining primaries. Besides, in many states, it was too late to become an official candidate.

McCarthy and Kennedy each won crucial primaries. McCarthy won an important victory in the May 28 Oregon primary. Kennedy followed with a win in the California primary on June 4, but was assassinated leaving his victory rally at a Los Angeles hotel. Meanwhile, Humphrey had quietly secured the support of enough delegates to be assured of a victory at the convention. Humphrey obtained his delegates in states that did not hold primaries, the majority at the time, or in primary states where the preference ballots were not connected to delegate selection. Yet, Humphrey's nomination would lack legitimacy as the public began to increasingly view the primaries as an important avenue to voice their opinion on the candidates.[23] The 1968 Democratic convention held in Chicago proved to be a disaster for the party. Outside the convention, violence broke out between anti-war demonstrators and the Chicago police. Inside the convention, a floor fight over the party's platform position on the Vietnam War ended with the anti-war position losing. Disillusioned delegates marched and protested, a disruption televised to a nationwide audience.

McCarthy and Kennedy supporters felt that the delegate selection process had discriminated against them. One-third of the convention delegates had been chosen by the end of 1967, too early for those who would be drawn in to support one of the two anti-war candidates. Many of the states also used rules that allowed for delegate selection to be dominated by party veterans and some events were unpublicized to newcomers.[24] For example, in Georgia and Louisiana the governors selected all of their state's Democratic convention delegates. In eight other states, the party's state committees selected the delegations. In many states, no rules appeared to govern the selection of delegates.[25]

Even in the primary states, the popular vote for the candidates did not always determine the selection of the convention delegates. In Pennsylvania, only Eugene McCarthy's name was listed on the preference portion of the ballot, and he won 76 percent of the popular vote with the remainder being write-in votes for Hubert Humphrey and Robert Kennedy. Yet Pennsylvania's delegates were selected in a separate section of the ballot, where individuals ran to be delegates without listing their candidate preferences. In addition, one-third of Pennsylvania's delegates were simply appointed by the state party committee. As a result, 84 percent of Pennsylvania's convention delegates supported Hubert Humphrey while 76 percent of the voters had supported McCarthy.[26] With growing dissatisfaction over delegate selection rules, or lack of rules, at the end of the 1968 convention the Democratic Party voted to establish a commission to investigate the rules for delegate selection and to develop national standards.

The Democratic Commission on Party Structure and Delegate Selection, most commonly called the McGovern-Fraser Commission after its two chairs (first South Dakota senator George McGovern followed by Minnesota representative Donald Fraser), developed 18 guidelines that states would have to follow in order for their delegations to be seated at the 1972 convention. Among the major provisions were

1   A mandate to increase the demographic representativeness of state delegations along the lines of race, gender and age.

2   Rules that party meetings, such as local caucuses or state conventions, would need to follow if a state selected convention delegates through these methods. These rules cover items such as quorum requirements and the banning of proxy voting.
3   Requiring public notices of dates and sites of any meeting or primary at which convention delegates would be selected.
4   Requiring potential delegates to indicate their candidate preference or state that they were uncommitted.
5   Banning selection of any delegate before January 1 of the election year.
6   Forbidding automatic selection of party officials as ex officio delegates.
7   Allowing no more than 10 percent of delegates to be appointed by a committee.[27]

In general, two basic principles were highlighted. First, the delegate selection process must be open to any Democrat who wanted to participate. Nominating events must be publicized and conducted under open rules. Second, the process must be timely in that it occurred during the election year. The McGovern-Fraser Commissioners were aiming at a fairer delegate selection process, whether it was in a local caucus or a primary election. What happened instead is that the new rules led to a proliferation of presidential primaries. Many state party leaders concluded that it would be easiest to comply with the new rules through a primary. Other party leaders felt that a primary would isolate presidential politics from other state party business.[28]

The new Democratic Party rules were not the only reason that more states began to enact presidential primary laws. Media coverage of primaries in the 1950s and 1960s had given extra legitimacy to this process for selecting delegates. In addition, many states saw that media coverage of primaries gave those states free publicity. Candidates tromping through the New Hampshire snows were a free advertisement for its winter sports vacations. New party activists within the states also were demanding changes for greater participation and more intraparty democracy.[29]

The resulting growth in the number of presidential primaries is illustrated in Figure 1.1, while the percent of each party's convention delegates selected through these primaries is given in Figure 1.2. In 1968, 15 states held presidential primaries choosing 40 percent of the delegates. Even if a candidate swept all the primaries, he would not have a sufficient number of delegate votes at the convention based on these primary victories alone. Not quite half of the states would hold presidential primaries in 1972, but these states now chose a majority of the convention delegates. In 1976, a majority of states would hold primaries, and they would select three out of four delegates. Thus, starting in the 1970s, candidates could

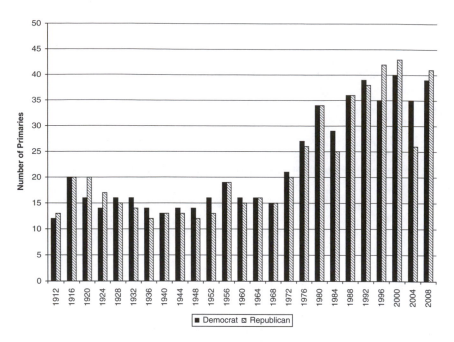

Figure 1.1 Number of primaries each year by party.

Source: *Guide to U.S. Elections,* 5th edition, volume 1 (Washington, DC: CQ Press, 2005), p. 318, updated by author.

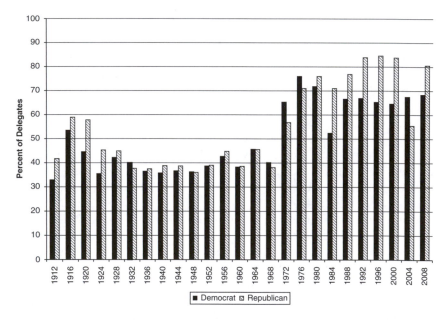

Figure 1.2 Percent of convention delegates selected through primaries by year and party.

Source: *Guide to U.S. Elections,* 5th edition, volume 1, p. 318, updated by author.

win sufficient numbers of delegates in the primary states to secure the presidential nomination.

Since 1980, an average of 36 primaries are held in any year, selecting two-thirds of the Democratic delegates and nearly 80 percent of the Republican delegates. (The smaller percentage of Democratic delegates selected through primaries since 1984 is due to the party's use of super-delegates, which are unpledged elected and party officials.) The decline in the number of presidential primaries in 2004 came as a handful of states eliminated presidential primaries in the face of tight state budgets. Holding a presidential primary costs states millions of dollars. The even greater decline on the Republican side was due to the lack of any challengers to President Bush's renomination, leading a few more states to cancel their Republican primaries. In 2008, the number of presidential primaries returned to an average level with 39 Democratic and 41 Republican contests which selected 68 percent of the Democratic delegates and 81 percent of the Republican delegates.

In most states, if a primary is used for one party it is used for the other. But every year a small number of states have separate procedures for each party. For example, in 2008 Idaho Democrats selected their delegates through a caucus, while Idaho Republicans used a primary. Also, in a small number of cases, the date of delegate selection varies across the two parties. The Democratic Party in New Mexico in 2008 sponsored its own presidential primary on February 5, while the Republican Party used the official state primary held on June 3.

The Democratic Party continued to have a series of reform commissions in the 1970s and 1980s. They debated rules concerning the allocation of convention delegates to match voter preferences, who should be allowed to participate in the Democratic Party presidential nominations, whether delegates should be legally bound to support a particular candidate at the convention, which dates to allow delegate selection to occur, and how to ensure a more demographically representative convention. We will return to these questions in Chapter 3.

So far, the story on presidential nomination reform in the mid-20th century has focused on the Democratic Party. This reform era did play out more within the Democratic Party, just as the Progressive reform era of the early 20th century unfolded more within Republican circles. The Republican Party in the 1960s and 1970s established two reform commissions that dealt with questions such as opening up the caucuses and state convention processes, banning proxy voting, abolishing ex officio delegates, and ensuring the selection of more female delegates. Yet, generally less demand existed for reforms within the Republican Party at this time. The party was not as divided over issues as were the Democrats, nor did the Republican Party have outdated convention rules such as the unit rule. The Republican Party also maintains a structure that allows individual state parties more autonomy. Finally, Republican Party rules were more difficult to change, requiring changes in delegate selection rules to be approved by the prior national convention.[30]

Changes in delegate selection rules in the mid-20th century, the Progressive reforms which introduced primaries in the early years of that century, and the abandonment of presidential nomination by congressional caucus in the early 19th century all followed a similar reform cycle format.[31] The first stage of this nomination reform cycle begins with a growing concern that existing procedures are unfair. In the 1820s the congressional caucuses were increasingly seen as unrepresentative, not allowing a voice for the growing party structure in the states. In the 1910s the political conventions were seen as dominated by corrupt party officials and did not provide a mechanism for a public voice. In the 1960s the voice that the public did have in selecting convention delegates was viewed as inadequate. In the second stage of the reform cycle, a crisis brings these lingering concerns to the forefront, whether it was the nomination of four Democratic-Republican candidates for president in 1824 or the rancor at the 1968 Democratic convention. The third stage is to put into place a set of reforms: a switch to a political convention, the enactment of presidential primaries, or a party commission issuing national rules for delegate selection. The fourth stage is the reaction to the new rules and perhaps a backlash. The Democratic Party continued to modify its rules after the McGovern-Fraser Commission, and even reversed itself on the ban on automatic selection of party officials as delegates. Yet, each new nominating system maintains a core set of reforms.

These series of reforms, from the 1830s to the 1980s, have changed the locus of control over presidential nominations. The switch from the congressional caucuses to the political conventions in the 1830s moved the center of party power over presidential nominations from the national to the state parties. The reform movement of the mid-20th century restored the ability of the national party to dictate to the state parties, and state governments, the rules for presidential nominations. Today, the national parties set the rules for delegate selection, but the states continue to have leeway on the selection of primaries versus caucuses, dates of delegate selection, and within the Republican Party, methods of allocating delegates based on voters' candidate preferences.

The Primary-Dominated Era: 1972 and Forward

Presidential nominations in 2008 were conducted under the procedures started in the 1970s. With more than a majority of convention delegates selected through presidential primaries, candidates could now accumulate a winning total of delegates by entering these primaries. No longer were candidates entering primaries to demonstrate their electoral strength to the party regulars who made up the convention delegates. The primaries were now *the method* for candidates to have their own supporters selected as convention delegates. And with open and publicized caucuses, presidential contenders could also have their supporters selected as delegates in the remainder of the states. The public by voting in primaries and participating in caucuses would have a direct say in the selection of the Democratic and Republican candidates for president.

The candidates who would claim the Democratic and Republican nominations would become evident well before the party conventions, still held in late summer of each election year. When one candidate had enough of their supporters selected as delegates to constitute 50 percent of the convention total, that candidate would become the party's unofficial nominee. With the exception of the 2008 Democratic contests, the unofficial nominee is often known by the middle of March. At that time, one candidate has the required number of delegates, or nearly the required number of delegates. The remaining candidates have already dropped out of the contest, due to losses in early presidential primaries or because they lagged behind in delegate totals. Thus, in 2008 John McCain claimed the Republican mantle after Thompson, Giuliani, Romney, and Huckabee dropped out. Even Barack Obama secured the nomination at the beginning of June when the last of the presidential primaries were held.

Presidential nominations are still officially bestowed at the national conventions. The role of the convention, however, has switched from selecting the party's presidential nominee to unifying the party behind that nominee. At some point, the convention will have the traditional roll call of states to have a public announcement of delegate preferences. The totals for the winning candidate are often higher than those initially gained from primary victories, as candidates who withdrew from the race release their delegates who most often switch their allegiance to the presumptive nominee. At the 2008 Republican convention, John McCain received the support of 98 percent of the delegates. The roll call of states at the Democratic convention was halted at New York to allow Hillary Clinton to call for Barack Obama's nomination to be by acclamation, a motion that easily passed.

Today's conventions are well-orchestrated publicity events for the two parties. The goal is to show party unity and to have no convention surprises. The presumptive presidential nominee will have already announced his or her selection of a vice presidential candidate, typically in the week before the convention. The party platform has been prewritten by a committee, containing the issue positions of the party's nominee and, perhaps, a few concessions to the losing candidates. The convention schedule contains many short speeches, by elected officials such as governors or senators, or by interest groups associated with the party. One person is selected to give the convention's keynote address, a major speech intended to highlight the goals of the party. As previously noted, Barack Obama made his first major national speech giving the keynote address at the 2004 Democratic convention. On the second to last night of the convention, the vice presidential nominee gives her or his speech. The final night is reserved for the speech of the presidential nominee. At the close of the presidential candidate's speech, balloons drop from the convention hall ceiling, or in the case of Obama's outdoor speech in 2008, fireworks are set off. A successful convention will boost the nominee's numbers in the national polls by 6 percentage points, at least temporarily.[32]

Having recapped the history of presidential nomination politics in this first chapter, the next two chapters of the book will take a deeper look into the primary-dominated nomination process (Chapter 2) and its potential problems and biases (Chapter 3). Some feel that the current system is in need of additional reform, and Chapter 4 will investigate these plans. But as the history of presidential nomination demonstrates, the outcome of any new reform is hard to predict. Chapter 5 will conclude this discussion by highlighting the pluses and minuses of early 21st-century U.S. presidential nomination politics.

Chapter 2

Presidential Nomination Politics at the Dawn of the 21st Century

At first glance, each presidential nomination contest appears to be unique. Folklore develops on how certain instances or decisions were crucial to the battle being waged. One such example is the frequent retelling of the events from a Manchester, New Hampshire coffee shop in 2008 when an audience member asked Senator Hillary Clinton how she could continue to campaign given the on-going adversity (and a loss in the Iowa caucuses). Clinton replied, "It's not easy . . . . I couldn't do it if I just didn't passionately believe it was the right thing to do . . . I just don't want to see us fall backwards."[1] Did this wistful (or as depicted in some media accounts tearful) response turn the tide in the 2008 New Hampshire primary, leading to a Clinton come-back and setting up the long battle between Clinton and Senator Barack Obama? Did Howard Dean's scream at the conclusion of his pep talk to supporters after losing the 2004 Iowa caucuses doom his campaign? At other times, "Monday morning quarterbacks" criticize candidates for flaws in their strategies. For example, did Senator Bill Bradley's decision in 2000 to compete vigorously (and lose) in Iowa cause him to forfeit his early lead in New Hampshire?[2] Still others ask whether media bias distorts the outcome, such as questioning whether undue favorable coverage of McCain in 2000 or Obama in 2008 garnered them additional support at the polls.[3]

Presidential nomination battles have lots of intricacies because there are so many factors involved: numerous candidates, primaries and caucuses across the 50 states (and several territories), different rules for the two parties, an ever-changing calendar, and the impact of new technology. Each year a new group of candidates decides to seek their party's presidential nomination. Some are well known, some are not. Some have a better chance of winning the nomination bid than others. Neither a uniform set of primary rules nor a standardized calendar of dates exist, because primary dates and rules are governed by the national parties, state parties, and state governments. These three groups often have competing rather than complementary interests. Presidential campaigns also are altered as candidates learn to exploit the latest technological advances. In 2000,

McCain opened up the internet as a fundraising tool. In 2004, Howard Dean exploited social networking to bring his supporters to key campaign events. By 2008, internet fundraising and social networking were key components to all the candidates' strategies.

Recent Nomination Contests

Despite the intricacies of each nomination contest, much commonality exists. In many races there is a frontrunner—someone who leads in the early public opinion polls and has raised a large amount of money. Sometimes this frontrunner has a commanding lead and goes on to win the nomination. In a less common scenario, the frontrunner falters and is replaced by another candidate. A third category is a contest with no clear frontrunner but a number of more equal contenders vying for the nomination. In yet another variant, two strong competitors may battle it out over the entire course of the presidential primaries and caucuses. A final category includes sitting presidents seeking renomination. This is the most successful path to the nomination, because since the start of the 20th century, no sitting president seeking renomination has been defeated for the party's presidential slot. A few presidents, however, have had significant challenges to their renominations.[4] Let's see how the last three nomination cycles played out.

2000 Republicans and Democrats: Frontrunner Victories

The 2000 Republican nomination is a clear case of a strong frontrunner winning the nomination. Texas governor George W. Bush established a commanding lead in fundraising totals and public opinion polls in 1999. In January 2000 Bush won the Iowa caucuses over his five competitors. New Hampshire proved to be a tougher fight. Arizona senator John McCain campaigned extensively in the state. Between April 1999 and January 2000, McCain held 114 town meetings in New Hampshire, often taking audience questions for up to 90 minutes.[5] McCain's grassroots campaigning paid off with a New Hampshire victory. Bush recovered with a critical victory in South Carolina, and on Super Tuesday Bush won victories in seven primary states while McCain won in four mostly smaller states. As a result of his victories, Bush had accumulated 681 of the 1,034 delegates needed for the nomination while McCain's total stood at 225. Two days later, McCain conceded the race to Bush. On that date, March 9, George W. Bush became the presumptive nominee, though he would not become the legal nominee until confirmed as such on August 3 at the Republican National Convention in Philadelphia.

On the Democratic side in 2000, a frontrunner won the nomination even more easily. Vice President Al Gore swept the primaries and caucuses over his sole competitor former New Jersey senator Bill Bradley. As a sitting vice president, Gore had many advantages including nearly universal name recognition and access to the party's activists and campaign contributors. Not all former vice presidents are automatically successful in their quests for the presidential nomination, as the case of Dan Quayle shows. Gore, however, was judged a particularly successful vice president, who had worked well with President Clinton. Within the Democratic Party, President Clinton maintained high approval, and he heartily endorsed Gore's candidacy. Overcoming Gore's advantages would be an uphill battle, and many possible contenders simply decided not to run. Thus, Bradley became the sole opponent to Gore. Bradley had been a hardworking senator for 18 years, but he was a loner, did not connect well with other party officials, and was not an exciting speaker on the campaign trail.[6] Gore won decisively in the Iowa caucuses, and survived Bradley's strongest challenge in New Hampshire. Gore won all 11 primaries on Super Tuesday, March 7, and Bradley bowed out of the contest on March 9.

2004 Democrats: Switching Places

The Democratic presidential nomination contest in 2004 saw the front-runner, Howard Dean, overtaken by John Kerry in the Iowa caucuses. Dean's frontrunner status was not insurmountable from the beginning. He led in funds raised in 2003 by $16 million over John Kerry (a relatively small lead compared to Bush's $34 million advantage at the same time in 1999). In addition, Dean had only taken the first-place slot in the national public opinion polls in October 2003. By late fall of 2003, Dean's fortunes began to wane while Kerry's began to rise. Dean had risen to early prominence among the Democratic contenders by criticizing the Iraq War, but on December 14, Saddam Hussein was captured, and public support for the war rose in response. Meanwhile, Senator John Kerry took out a $6.4 million mortgage on his home to help finance his campaign. This presented a mixed message. On the one hand, resorting to the use of personal funds may signal a crisis within a campaign unable to attract enough support from campaign contributors, but on the other hand, the size of Kerry's personal loan sent a cue as to his seriousness about the campaign and allowed him to hire more staff.

Dean had other weaknesses in his Iowa campaign, such as relying on out-of-state rather than local volunteers, and Kerry had hidden strengths, with support among Iowa's veterans and firefighters. Kerry also had the good fortune that Jim Rassmann, a Vietnam veteran, stepped forward to credit Kerry with saving his life during the war. Rassmann began to actively campaign with Kerry in Iowa. Dean's main competitor in Iowa had been Dick Gephardt, the Missouri congressman who needed to win in his own region. As caucus night neared, Gephardt and Dean began to question each other's electability. The tug of war between Dean and Gephardt took its toll. Meanwhile, John Edwards also was gaining in Iowa with upbeat speeches and the endorsement of the *Des Moines Register*.[7]

On caucus night, January 19, Kerry won the support of 38 percent of the caucus attendees, Edwards finished second at 32 percent, with Dean at 18 percent, and Gephardt at 11 percent. Dean's misfortunes in Iowa were augmented with a post-caucus speech before 3,500 supporters. In his rousing speech, Dean ticked off upcoming primary states he expected to win, pledged to take back the White House for the Democrats, and ended with a vociferous shout of "Yeeeeaaaaah!" On the television news, late-night talk shows, and the internet, Dean's scream appeared to show the candidate as desperate and angry. Kerry's momentum took over. Dean's 30-point lead in New Hampshire disappeared, and on primary night, Kerry bested Dean 39 to 26 percent.[8] Kerry went on to win 15 of the 18 primaries held between February 3 and March 2, forcing the remaining candidates from the contest, and unofficially securing the Democratic nomination.

2004 Republicans: A Presidential Renomination

The 2004 Republican nomination battle was nonexistent. President George W. Bush was not challenged in his bid to be renominated. The last serious challenge to a sitting president by a credible candidate was in 1980, when Senator Edward Kennedy opposed Jimmy Carter's renomination. Carter's presidency was plagued by the stagnant economy of the 1970s and rising gas prices in 1979. Yet, Kennedy was unable to articulate why he would be a better contender, and the early rally-around-the-flag boost in Carter's approval ratings from the taking of the U.S. embassy personnel in Iran in November 1979 helped Carter stave off Kennedy's challenge. In 1976, the unelected presidency of Gerald Ford (he assumed the presidency when Richard Nixon stepped down due to the Watergate scandal) was challenged by the party's conservative leader, former California governor Ronald Reagan. Ford and Reagan traded primary victories, and neither controlled a majority of the delegates at the close of the last primaries. Ford gained the final few delegates needed over the course of the summer, but was renominated by the slimmest of margins with 52.5 percent of the delegates.[9]

Other recent presidents have not faced such serious opposition to their renomination. In 1992, President George H. W. Bush faced an ideological challenge from political commentator Patrick Buchanan. A protest vote from conservatives upset that Bush had broken his no new taxes pledge helped Buchanan move within 16 points of Bush in the New Hampshire primary. Buchanan remained a critic of Bush throughout the rest of the campaign, though he would not win any of the primaries. President Bill Clinton was unchallenged for renomination in 1996 as was Ronald Reagan in 1984. Thus, in the past quarter century, only two presidents have faced serious challengers, one an ideological challenge, and three were unopposed for their renomination. Wayne Steger in studying challenges to sitting presidents in the 20th century concludes that presidents are most likely to face a serious challenger when the president is unpopular with a significant faction of the party but the party still has a reasonable chance of winning the fall election.[10] Nonetheless, Ford, Carter, and George H. W. Bush all lost their reelection bids.

2008 Republicans: Who's the Frontrunner?

The 2008 Republican contest presented mixed evidence on frontrunner status. Former New York City mayor Rudy Giuliani led in the national polls throughout 2007. As mayor of New York City at the time of the 9/11 terrorists' attacks, Giuliani campaigned on his record of being tough on terrorists, but his more colorful personal life and moderate stances on social issues did not sit well with party conservatives. Mitt Romney, the former governor of Massachusetts, led in campaign finances, though one-third came from his own personal fortune. Despite the credentials of being a successful Republican governor in a Democratic state, Romney had recently adopted more conservative positions on social issues and faced lingering prejudices against his Mormon faith. John McCain's campaign was financially broke by the summer of 2007. With a reduced staff, McCain began a fall "No Surrender" bus tour to regain his grassroots support. In addition, McCain's early advocacy of a larger U.S. military force in the Iraq War began to resonate with Republican voters, and he performed well in the Republican candidate debates. McCain's position in the national polls moved upwards by the end of 2008, as did that of Mike Huckabee, whose congenial ways and conservative positions on social issues captured the support of the party's religious faction. Yet, no candidate seemed poised to unify the various types of conservatives within the Republican Party: religious conservatives, economic conservatives, and foreign policy conservatives.

The 2008 election season opened with Huckabee winning the Iowa caucuses. Romney who had campaigned heavily in the state finished second. McCain, who had skipped Iowa (a tactic more successful in the Republican than Democratic Party), won in New Hampshire. Once again, Romney finished second, but he won the Michigan primary and caucuses in Nevada and Maine. Fred Thompson, the former Tennessee senator and actor, claimed to be focusing on the South Carolina primary. When he finished third, he left the race. Giuliani proclaimed he was waiting for the Florida primary to demonstrate his strengths, but finishing third, exited the race and endorsed McCain. By Super Tuesday only Romney, Huckabee, McCain, and Ron Paul, an advocate for libertarian policies, remained in the Republican fray. McCain's victory in 9 of the 15 Republican Super Tuesday primaries led Romney to quit the race, while Huckabee waited another month until McCain could claim the support of 50 percent of the Republican delegates, the number needed for victory, before dropping out. By the beginning of March, John McCain had secured enough delegates to claim the Republican nomination and forced all of the serious contenders from the field.

2008 Democrats: A Two-Candidate Battle

The 2008 Democratic nomination sure appeared to break the mold. The two leading candidates were a woman, Senator Hillary Rodham Clinton of New York, and an African American, Senator Barack Obama of Illinois. Six other candidates also were in the race, did poorly in the early contests, and by the end of January most of these had quit the race. Clinton and Obama, however, would vie for the nomination throughout the entire presidential primary and caucus calendar. The last extended primary contest was more than 20 years previous, when Senator Gary Hart and former vice president Walter Mondale contested the 1984 Democratic nomination. In 2008, Obama would win in Iowa, Clinton in New Hampshire. The vote on Super Tuesday was split. Clinton was unprepared for a longer battle (most pundits had predicted the race would be over on Super Tuesday) and did not intend to spend much time or effort contesting the caucuses (few candidates in the past had done so). Obama won a string of caucuses and primaries in February. Clinton came back with a win in the March 4 Ohio, Texas, and Rhode Island primaries, while Obama won in the Vermont primary and the caucus portion of the Texas selection. The two candidates evenly split the remaining 10 primaries, but with the help of superdelegates Obama's delegate total exceeded the 50 percent mark on the last primary day. Clinton conceded the contest the following Saturday.

Long battles for the presidential nomination had become rare over the past quarter century. The other two instances date back to the 1984 Democratic contest (between Vice President Walter Mondale and Colorado senator Gary Hart) and the 1976 Republican battle (between Ford and Reagan). All three occurrences involve a protracted battle between two candidates, rather than a multicandidate contest. John Aldrich theorizing about the course of presidential nomination politics argues that only the two-candidate scenario is likely to produce a long extended campaign.[11] Each candidate will have his or her ups and downs. When one candidate gains, the other falls behind, but then the tide turns and the roles are switched. As long as each candidate has her or his strengths, and weaknesses, the relatively balanced contest continues to the end of the primary season.

Multicandidate contests often end more quickly. Candidates who do not do well in the early primaries and caucuses drop out of the race. Those who do better in the early contests or have sufficient campaign resources continue to the next round of primaries and caucuses. In rare instances, the battle will dwindle to two main competitors who compete over time, as was the case in the 1984 and 2008 Democratic contests. Yet, a quicker and more common scenario for the conclusion of a multicandidate race is for one competitor to dominate the early contests, as happened with Kerry and the Democrats in 2004 and Bush and the Republicans in 2000. Sometimes the initial round may have two or three candidates win in different primaries and caucuses, but then one of the candidates puts together a series of wins. The rest of the candidates fall behind in resources and delegate totals, and quit the race. Thus, the most common dynamic of multicandidate contests is that they dwindle down to a single, winning candidate, though it may be hard to predict in some years (Democrats in 2004, Republicans in 2008) which of the initial set of candidates will be the successful one.

So far we have seen the different scenarios for nomination contests and how they have been highlighted in the first three election years of the 21st century. Next we will look at the basic elements to all these campaigns: 1) the emergence of the candidate field, 2) the pre-election year or "invisible primary" battle for name recognition and campaign resources, 3) the election year dynamics of momentum and candidate attrition, and 4) the accumulation of delegates, the key to the legal definition of winning the nomination.

The Candidates

Through the mid-20th century an unwritten list of criteria described the desired qualifications for a presidential nominee. This "availability standard" required the potential candidate to be a senator or a governor, preferably from a large, competitive state. Of course, that the candidate would be a white male was a given, as was the requirement that he be a Protestant and have an ideal marriage.[12] Gradually these standards were violated and went by the wayside as small-state (Eisenhower), Catholic (Kennedy), and divorced (Reagan) candidates won the presidency. Yet until 2008, all the winning candidates remained white males, and most serious contenders continued to be current or former senators and governors.

Senators, governors, and vice presidents have the name recognition, practical experience in campaigning, and a credible record of prior experience in governing to make good presidential candidates. Barry Burden, in investigating presidential candidates from 1960 to 2004, found the largest number (37 percent) were senators, followed by governors (22 percent). Yet, governors were more successful than senators at ultimately winning the nominations. In fact before 2008, the last sitting senator to win the White House was John Kennedy in 1960, though several senators were their party's nominees. Senators may be disadvantaged as presidential candidates because they often have a lengthy voting record that may be turned against them, and the greater number of senators running may mean that the list contains more mediocre candidates than the shorter list of gubernatorial contenders. Of course, presidents seeking renomination and vice presidents in quest of their own bids were particularly successful at winning the nomination.[13]

Candidates vying in the first three nomination cycles of the 21st century did not deviate much from the career paths of the candidates in previous decades, as the listings in Table 2.1 show. Senators were the most typical candidates, but a good number of governors ran as well. Breaking a bit from past patterns, senators were equally as likely as governors to ultimately win their party's presidential bid. Thus the victors in these three election cycles were Texas governor George W. Bush, Vice President Al Gore (and former Tennessee senator), Massachusetts senator John Kerry, Arizona senator John McCain, and Illinois senator Barack Obama.

Six candidates tried for the presidency from a current or former post in the House of Representatives, though most were considered second-tiered

Table 2.1 Last office held by candidates, 2000–2008

	Individuals who ran	% in each category	Success rate for each category
President	Bush	1 (3%)	100%
Vice President	Gore	1 (3%)	100%
Governor	Bush, Dean, Romney, Huckabee, Richardson	5 (14%)	20%
Senator	Bradley, McCain (2), Hatch, Smith, Edwards (2), Kerry, Lieberman, Thompson, Obama, Clinton, Biden, Dodd, Gravel	15 (43%)	20%
Representative	Kasich, Gephardt, Kucinich (2), Hunter, Paul	6 (17%)	0%
Other	Forbes, Keyes (2), Clark, Sharpton, Giuliani, Bauer	7 (20%)	0%

Note: List includes candidates who remained in the race at least until the Iowa caucuses. N = 35; success rate = # nominees/# contenders. Numbers in parentheses indicate a candidate ran multiple times in these years.

candidates due to lower visibility and fundraising totals. Some fit the mold of issue advocacy candidates, who use the presidential campaign to spread specific political messages or to advocate for core constituency groups. Thus, in 2008 Republican California representative Duncan Hunter ran on the issue of border security, and Republican Texas representative Ron Paul espoused a libertarian approach to conservatism. Only Richard Gephardt, the leader of the Democratic Party in the House, was considered a strong contender for the presidency, and his unsuccessful 2004 bid was his second try at the White House. Besides the lower visibility of House members to senators, all House members are up for reelection during presidential election years, while senators often run for the presidency in years they are not seeking reelection.

Among candidates from other positions in the 2000–2008 election cycles, the strongest contender was former New York City mayor Rudy Giuliani. As mayor of New York City during the 9/11 attacks Giuliani had the level of name recognition often found for the more famous senators. A flawed campaign strategy of avoiding the initial contests for a decisive victory in the Florida primary imploded when Giuliani finished third in that contest. Wesley Clark was a retired four-star Army general when he ran for the 2004 Democratic nomination, and his inexperience in electoral politics led to amateurish mistakes.[14] Meanwhile, Gary Bauer served in the Reagan administration and with various religiously conservative interest groups. Alan Keyes also served in the Reagan administration and as a political commentator. His 2008 bid was his third try at the presidency, and he also failed three times to win a seat in the U.S. Senate. Finally, Al Sharpton is a civil rights activist and political commentator. These last three fit the mold of issue advocacy candidacies, using the campaign to spread a specific message, rather than having a realistic chance of winning the nomination.

Two women other than Hillary Clinton declared themselves as candidates for president in the past three election cycles, both leaving the race before the first ballots were cast. (A number of male candidates also announced plans to run for president but withdrew before the first primary.[15]) Elizabeth Dole sought the Republican presidential nomination in 2000. She was the former head of the Red Cross and had served as both the Secretary of Labor and Secretary of Transportation in the Reagan administration. Yet, Dole had never run for public office before. While she scored high in the national public opinion polls, she was unable to translate this into a successful fundraising organization. Some analysts also report Dole did not receive as much media coverage as her poll standings would warrant and that the coverage she did receive paid more attention to her personality and appearance.[16] Dole withdrew from the race on October 20, 1999. Carol Moseley Braun was the first female

African American senator, but she served only one term representing the state of Illinois. She withdrew from the 2004 Democratic contest on January 15, citing a lack of funds and name recognition.

Three other women have been candidates for the two major parties' presidential nomination and two have been the vice presidential nominees. In 1972, Shirley Chisholm, the first African American woman to serve in Congress, garnered 3 percent of the vote in the Democratic primaries. In 1976, Ellen McCormack ran as a pro-life candidate in the Democratic primaries, winning 2 percent of the vote. Maine senator Margaret Chase Smith was the first woman to have her name formally placed in the bid for a major party's presidential nomination, when she received nominal support at the 1964 Republican convention. In 1984, New York representative Geraldine Ferraro was the first woman nominated by a major party for the vice presidential slot. She joined former vice president Walter Mondale on the Democratic ticket. Thus, Alaska governor Sarah Palin was the second female vice presidential candidate.

Before 2007, no woman had been a frontrunner for a major party's presidential nomination. Hillary Clinton would be the first to do so. Still, as a woman she faced obstacles that her male colleagues did not. The words that we use to describe a president are those we often associate with men, such as being tough and assertive, while women are stereotyped as compassionate and passive.[17] Female leaders in many fields beyond politics face the bias of either being perceived as competent but cold or less competent but kindly.[18] Thus Clinton worked hard to build an image consonant with our expectations for a president. She was successful. The public perceived her as qualifying to be the nation's commander-in-chief, but at the same time, Clinton struggled against the image that she was cold and calculating.

Barack Obama also was not the first African American to run for a major party's presidential nomination. Alan Keyes sought the support of religious conservatives in his bids for the Republican nomination. Other African American candidates have vied for the Democratic slot. As mentioned previously, two African American women sought the Democratic nomination: Shirley Chisholm and Carol Moseley Braun. In 2004, Al Sharpton, a minister and civil rights activist, ran in the Democratic primaries, but won only 2.4 percent of the vote. Prior to Obama, the most successful African American candidate was Jesse Jackson, also a minister and civil rights activist. In 1984, Jackson won 18 percent of the primary vote. In 1988, Jackson finished second among all candidates, winning seven primaries and four caucuses. Jackson's strategy was to create a "Rainbow Coalition" of minority, poor, and liberal voters. Jackson won primaries in states where a large proportion of the Democratic electorate was African Americans and in caucuses where liberal whites were a larger proportion of the attendees. However, in the last round of primaries, when the race narrowed to Michael Dukakis versus Jackson, Dukakis won all but one primary by a two-to-one margin. The exception was the Washington, DC primary. Thus, before 2008, no African American candidate had been able to expand his or her base to win the support of a large number of white voters.

Sometimes the contest is decided not so much by what the candidates do as by who decides not to run. If former vice president Al Gore had decided to run for the Democratic nomination in 2008, he may have cut into Hillary Clinton's base. A leading contender for the 1992 Democratic nomination was New York governor Mario Cuomo, until he formally announced he would not run late in December 1991. Similarly in 1995, former general Colin L. Powell, Jr. was a frontrunner in public opinion polls for the Republican nomination, but he declared on November 8 that he would not run.

We know that the typical presidential nominee will be a senator, governor, or vice president. We are less able to tell which of these types of politicians will actually run for the presidency. Even those candidates who declare their intentions to run do not know exactly who their competitors may be. Some politicians wait until fairly late to officially declare their quest for the nomination, though they may have been more quietly sizing up their chances of winning. Some people expected to run decide not to. Other politicians might declare they are running at an earlier point, but finding out they lacked support or resources quit the race before the first primary. The number of candidates running for the presidential nominations also varies widely. If a president is seeking renomination, he or she is likely to face few challengers. In the opposition party, the number of declared candidates may be six, seven, or even more. Who finally runs and who becomes a strong candidate are two factors often established during the invisible primary season.

The (Not So) Invisible Primary

The year (or two) leading up to the presidential election is awash with campaign activities. Various candidates test the waters, making preliminary excursions to early primary and caucus states, forming exploratory committees to test their ability to raise campaign funds, and conducting their own public opinion polls to uncover what the public likes and dislikes about them. In 1976, journalist Arthur Hadley coined the phrase the "invisible primary" to describe this pre-election year activity.[19] While some journalists and party activists pay attention to these initial candidate efforts, most Americans give little heed to this early stage of the competition. Only when the election year arrives and candidates run in the primaries and caucuses does the general public become interested. Yet, the invisible primary is no longer so hidden. In part because of the front-loading of the primary calendar and the greater need for early money and name recognition, candidate activities in the pre-election year have become more visible. Even the structure of this campaigning has changed. In 2007, more than a dozen candidate debates were held on each side of the partisan divide: 17 for the Democratic candidates and 15 among the Republican contenders. The goal of candidate activity in the pre-election year stage is to garner the resources, in terms of money, endorsements, and public recognition, that will facilitate victories in the election-year primaries and caucuses.

Gathering the Money

From the 1970s through the 1990s, the fundraising strategies of the candidates were molded by the campaign finance laws established by the Federal Election Campaign Act (FECA) of 1971 and modified in 1974 and 1976 with amendments. This legislation set up contribution limits (originally $1,000 per person but in 2008, $2,300) for all candidates seeking federal (e.g., president, Congress) offices. In reaction to the Watergate scandal, the 1974 legislation set up a system for public (i.e., government) funding of presidential elections. For the fall presidential election, the federal government would provide a set sum of money to the Democratic and Republican candidates, and these candidates would be limited to using these funds for their campaigns. In 1976 it was $20 million; in 2008 it was $84 million (only McCain accepted this).

For the primary phase of the presidential election, candidates may seek to qualify for federal matching funds by first raising $100,000. These funds must be raised in a way to demonstrate a wide appeal. Thus, to qualify for federal matching funds a candidate must raise $5,000 in contributions of $250 or less in 20 states. Once a candidate qualifies for matching funds, the federal government matches one-for-one the first $250 of a contribution from an individual donor. The money for the federal matching funds system comes from a voluntary $3 check-off on the federal income tax form. Money from interest groups, in the form of political action committees (PACs), is not matched, and this established a pattern that PACs contribute less than 5 percent of the money raised for the presidential nominations. Once a candidate accepts the matching funds from the government, the candidate is limited in the amount of money that can be spent in each state, and the entire amount that can be spent nationwide. In 2008 this nationwide limit was $42 million.

With one exception (John Connally in 1980), all major candidates for the presidential nomination accepted federal matching funds through 1992 even though accepting federal funds limited campaign strategies. Individual state limits could be circumvented to some extent with accounting tricks, such as renting the cars used in the New Hampshire primary campaign in Boston rather than Manchester. The overall national limits were more of a hindrance to successful candidates. In 1996, Bob Dole spent most of his allowed money to win the nomination, leaving him no money for campaigning during the summer months before the Republican convention.[20]

In 1996, self-financed candidate Steve Forbes used mostly his own money ($37 million) to run his campaign, and thus, was not subject to the spending limits for any particular primary. This allowed him to spend more heavily in individual states. In 2000, George W. Bush declined government matching funds. Steve Forbes ran a second time, again spending mostly his own money. George Bush's $60 million raised in 1999 was seen as an astonishing feat and gave him enough money to vigorously campaign in every state and to come back from the setback of losing in New Hampshire. By 2004, both Howard Dean and John Kerry declined the government funding. In 2008, few serious candidates accepted matching funds and the spending restrictions that went along with them.[21] The largest amount of federal money went to John Edwards, $12.8 million, which was 22 percent of his $58.4 million total. Edwards's acceptance of federal funds was seen as a sign of weakness in his campaign.

Most of the money, even for candidates accepting federal matching funds, comes from contributions from individual Americans. Candidates have several strategies for raising these funds. Fundraising events, such as dinners, cocktail parties, or other gatherings, are used to attract initial donors or contributions from more wealthy donors who can contribute the maximum amount (again, $2,300 in 2008). Campaigns also employ networking, eliciting wealthy individuals to make their own contributions but also to contact their friends and acquaintances to make contributions. In the 1980s and 1990s, candidates wanting to solicit small contributions resorted to direct mail tactics, which are expensive and slow, or set up a 1-800 number. By 2000, the internet had supplanted these techniques, and candidates could now cheaply and quickly raise campaign funds in small sums from a large number of people.

Figure 2.1 shows how the 2000–2008 major candidates raised their campaign funds. The sums are divided into three time periods: the invisible primary (pre-election year), the competitive primary stage (usually through Super Tuesday), and the post-competitive primary phase (e.g., a quasi-general election period where one presumptive nominee begins to campaign against the opposite party's presumptive nominee). In the graph for 2000, Bush's commanding lead in fundraising during the invisible primary stage is very apparent. He raised more in the year before the election than McCain did during the entire election cycle. Most of McCain's fundraising came early in the election year, when he was doing well in New Hampshire, but even then he could not catch up to Bush's totals. Steve Forbes's numbers included mostly his own money. The Democratic "money primary" in 2000 was more evenly matched. Gore and Bradley raised similar amounts at similar time intervals. A significant proportion of

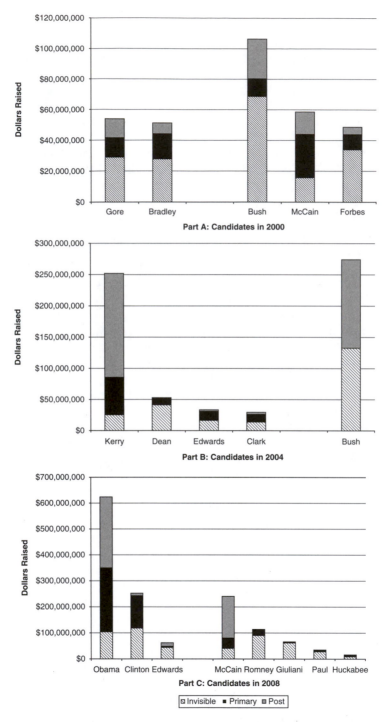

Figure 2.1 Candidate fundraising by period, 2000–2008.

Source: Federal Election Commission.

the post-competitive primary money for these two candidates was the awarding of the government matching funds, which lags behind money coming in from individual contributors. Bush's post-competitive primary fundraising enabled him to start the fall campaign against Gore during the spring and summer months. This was a definite advantage over Gore who had accepted federal matching funds and was subject to an overall limit in spending. Because of the edge Bush gained in the quasi-fall election campaign, fewer candidates in the next two election cycles would accept federal matching funds and their limits.

In 2004, the largest proportion of Kerry's money was in the post-competitive phase, after he secured the nomination and was beginning the quasi-fall election campaign in March. Early fundraising showed a lead for Dean, but not by much. Kerry once he started to win the early contests also garnered more money, making it even more difficult for other candidates to remain competitive. Even though President Bush had no competition in the 2004 primary phase, he could raise private funds. In Figure 2.1, his totals are simply divided into that raised in the pre-election year and that raised in the election year. His campaign was able to use this money for the quasi-general election campaign against Kerry in the spring and summer of 2004.

By 2008, most of the major candidates were no longer accepting the government matching funds, so they could raise as much money as possible in every phase of the competition. This money is overwhelmingly private contributions from individual Americans, and more of it is now coming over the internet. Some of the money raised by candidates is in large contributions, close to the $2,300 maximum and some of it is in small contributions of less than $200. About 50 percent of Clinton's early money was in large contributions and another 25 percent in sums over $1,000. Only 33 percent of Obama's early funds were at the maximum level, and 32 percent came in amounts of less than $200, as did 14 percent of Clinton's. With a larger number of small donors, Obama could resolicit more of his contributors later in the primary season. Clinton's campaign, despite the large sums raised, became strapped for cash at crucial stages in the campaign, and she gave her campaign two personal loans that totaled to $11.4 million. Overall, both Clinton and Obama were highly successful campaign fundraisers, and this helped to foster the long nomination battle between the two.

Money raised during the 2007 invisible primary stage on the Republican side was even less predictive of the ultimate outcome. Romney raised $90.1 million but $35.4 million was his own money.[22] Giuliani raised $61 million, and McCain raised only $40 million. Further McCain over-spent during the early months of 2007, and he had only $3 million in cash-on-hand at the end of December. Some scholars have found that it is the December cash-on-hand figures that best predict the winning candidate in the presidential primaries, but the Republicans in 2008 were certainly an exception to this pattern.[23]

The quest for campaign funds during the invisible primary stage is certainly an important component of any presidential nomination. In many years, the frontrunner in campaign funds does win the nomination. The internet had democratized this quest for campaign funds. Most Americans can easily access candidates' webpages, and by 2008, the first screen encountered was a request for campaign funds. The internet replaced earlier attempts to equalize access to campaign funds through the use of the federal matching fund system. Yet, the internet will not replace all traditional methods of campaign fundraising, because candidates need to make a name for themselves before Americans will want to search for the webpages and make contributions.

Endorsements: The Voice of the Party Elite

The party elite still plays a role in presidential nominations, despite the dominance of presidential primaries for selecting delegates attached to the presidential candidates. The party's governors, senators, House members, and various other state and local government office holders may choose to endorse candidates during the invisible primary stage. Political scientists Marty Cohen, David Karol, Hans Noel, and John Zaller demonstrated that these endorsements are meaningful indicators of whether the party elite is coalescing behind a single candidate and making this candidate the frontrunner going into the primary election year.[24]

George W. Bush's 2000 campaign is their classic example of the party elite coordinating on a single candidate during the invisible primary season. Half of the Republican governors supported Bush's nomination in early 1999, and all but one would endorse him by the end of the year. Bush was the successful governor of Texas, and the Republican governors were pushing for the nomination of one of their own. Along with their endorsements, the governors introduced their key fundraisers and supporters to Bush. Other major Republican contributors also began to back Bush and help solicit still others to make contributions as well. In fact, Bush was able to do much of his early organization from Texas, as the party's elite flew to Austin to meet with him. All of this activity was a major reason that Bush was able to raise so much money during the invisible primary stage. But the process was about more than just money. Bush also was gaining the support of key leaders among the party's economic and religious wings. By the close of the invisible primary, not only was Bush endorsed by the party's governors, but he was the recipient of 65 percent of the endorsements from other party leaders. In contrast, John McCain had the second highest endorsement total, but at a mere 10 percent.[25]

Still, even if the party's elite coordinates behind a single candidate, that candidate must win the support of the party's voters in the caucuses and primaries.

The party elite does not always coordinate behind one candidate during the invisible primary season. In 2004, Cohen *et al.* found only 5 percent of the Democratic governors made an endorsement, and those that did split their support among several of the major candidates. With the party elite undecided, the early victories of John Kerry in Iowa and New Hampshire were significant in convincing both voters and the party elite to rally behind him. The Republican Party elite also were divided in 2008. None of the top three candidates, McCain, Giuliani, and Romney, was acceptable to leaders from all factions of the party. And none of these candidates was able to dominate among the early elite endorsements.[26] Without an elite consensus in these two years, the public voting in the primaries and caucuses became even more decisive in selecting the presidential nominee.

On the Democratic side in 2008, Hillary Clinton garnered much of the early support from party leaders in 2007, even the support of some of the party's African American leaders. Barack Obama had less of the early support among the party elite, because he was so new on the national scene with only two years of experience in the Senate. Yet, Obama did receive some significant early backing from important fundraisers, campaign professionals, and party activists. Still, many party elite, especially the elected officials, did not endorse Obama until after his initial caucus and primary victories. In 2008, the Democratic Party elite may have changed its mind midstream, but not until Obama proved his public popularity during the visible primary season.[27]

Early Public Preferences

The American public also has a voice during the invisible primary through the numerous public opinion polls taken during the pre-election year. The public's responses to the earliest polls, those taken a year or more before the election, reflect the preexisting national reputation of the candidates. Thus, the early stages of the preference polls reflect the name recognition of the candidates. Among those with high name recognition are national candidates from a previous election year, such as the party's previous presidential or vice presidential nominees. Sitting vice presidents and some senators also have high name recognition. Other candidates will need to build a base of support through speeches, rallies, or participation in candidate debates. Most of the public will not be paying close attention to these activities, but occasional news reports, especially if they consistently present positive information on a candidate, will filter through and begin to alter public preferences.

To see how these early public preferences played out in the 2000–2008 nomination battles, we will look at the responses to a Gallup poll question:

> I'm going to read a list of people who may be running in the [Republican/Democratic] primary for president in the next election. After I read all the names, please tell me which of those candidates you would be most likely to support for the [Republican/Democratic] nomination for president in the year [2000, etc.].[28]

The Gallup question continues with a listing of the major contenders. The relevant answers will be from those survey respondents who identify themselves as favoring one party over the other. Thus preferences for the Republican candidates will come from those respondents who say they are Republicans or independents that tend to favor the Republican Party. Likewise, preferences for the Democratic candidates will be shown from those respondents who identify themselves as Democrats or independents leaning toward the Democratic Party. These polling questions begin to be asked with some frequency about two years before the actual election.

The presidential nomination contests from 2000 to 2008 show three types of patterns in early public preferences and their relations to public opinion during the election year. Both the Democratic and Republican contests in 1999–2000 reveal a clear frontrunner during the invisible primary, as shown in Figure 2.2. Further, these early frontrunners kept their lead once the actual primary voting began. On the Republican side, Elizabeth Dole was in second place during the invisible primary, but she dropped out in October due to a lack of funds. John McCain's national support rose with his early primary victories, but he never came close to Bush's totals. On the Democratic side, Gore's advantage over Bradley in the invisible primary only grew larger in 2008 as Gore won in the primaries and Bradley did not. In these two election cycles, the public's preferences did not change much—the early leader maintained a commanding edge throughout the invisible and visible primary stages.

A different pattern is found for public preferences for the 2004 Democratic and 2008 Republican contests. The early phase is a jumble. The Democratic leader in 2003 was often Joe Lieberman, mostly because he was recognized as the party's vice presidential candidate from 2000. Kerry was close but faded in mid-2003. Wesley Clark took over first place when he entered the race but his support quickly fell off. The public was unsure of its preferences until Kerry won Iowa and New Hampshire, and then his support skyrocketed. The same thing happened for McCain in 2008. Once he started winning in the primaries, his support in the public opinion polls shot up. McCain, too, had a rough patch in the mid-section of the invisible primary stage before his support started to inch upward in late 2007. The Republican leader in 2007 was often Giuliani, buoyed

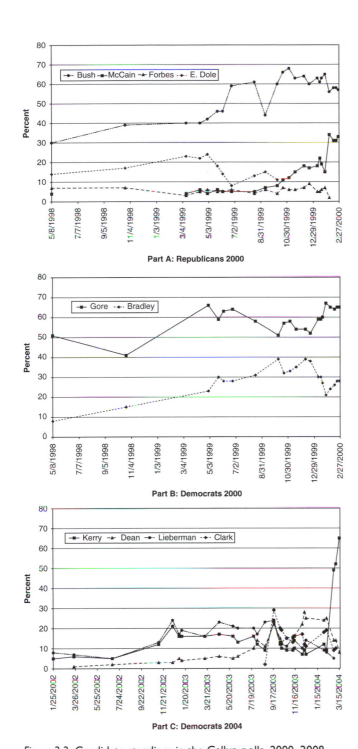

Figure 2.2 Candidate standings in the Gallup polls, 2000–2008.

Source: Gallup polls accessed through the Roper Center for Public Opinion Research, University of Connecticut.

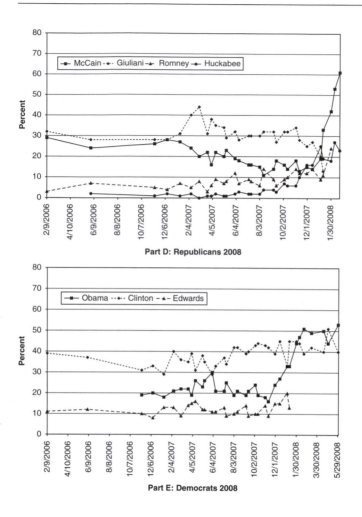

Figure 2.2 Cont'd

by his reputation as a strong leader after the 9/11 terrorist attack on New York City. But Giuliani failed to win in the actual primary contests in 2008. Huckabee and Romney did gain ground in late 2007 and during the early primaries, but failed to keep up with McCain. The mixed preferences during the invisible primary stages in these contests laid the stage for one candidate to take off during the primary phase by winning crucial early events.

The Democratic contest of 2008 presents a third pattern. Hillary Clinton clearly led in the invisible primary stage polls. For the most part, Clinton outpaced Obama by 10 percentage points or more. Clinton's support did not decline in 2008, but it did not grow by much either. Her support fluctuated between a bit below to a bit above 40 percent. Not quite the majority support that would lead to a nomination victory. This left the door open for Obama to gain support. After a steady state of 20 percent throughout most of 2007, Obama's support began to grow in the last two months of that year. His caucus and primary victories in early 2008 led to a quick upswing. Obama tied with Clinton in the national polls after Iowa, but Clinton retook the top spot after her win in New Hampshire. In early February Obama again led in the national polls, but Clinton briefly reclaimed the lead after her victory in the Pennsylvania primary. Finally, at the end of May and in the last stage of the visible primary season, Obama gained the support of 53 percent in the national public opinion polls. The 2008 Democratic race endured throughout the entire primary season because for the most part, Clinton held onto her base, which was quite substantial. Thus, Obama had to win over even more supporters to overtake Clinton's lead.

The national polls show three different types of contest: 1) a distinct frontrunner from the invisible primary stage who remains the frontrunner during the election year, 2) an invisible primary stage with no clear frontrunner, and when one candidate begins to win a number of the early primaries and caucuses, support for this candidate skyrockets, and 3) a candidate catching up with the initial frontrunner and eventually surpassing her. While there are three distinct patterns, all have one aspect in common. In all of these nominations, national public opinion reacted to the results of the primaries and caucuses. Success in the primaries affects the preferences of the party's supporters nationwide.

The Two-Tiered Nomination Process

Once the election year commences, two simultaneous processes determine the nomination outcomes. On one level is the national race: a competition between the candidates for a winning image. Candidates who do well in the primaries will gain in the national polls, or if they are a frontrunner, maintain their lead. Candidates who do well are often said to be gaining momentum, which gives them the assets to win subsequent events. Momentum candidates receive more coverage from the media, and this coverage is often positive. Momentum candidates also receive more campaign funds, and the internet allows them to garner these new campaign funds more quickly. Momentum also causes voters in future primaries to change their minds about the candidate, perhaps switching preferences from another candidate or more likely moving from a "don't know" stance to support for the advantaged candidate.[29] On the other side of the coin, candidates who do poorly drop out of the race. Thus, some voters have to change their minds because their preferred candidate is no longer in the race. The second competition is the delegate race. Through the primary and caucus results candidates accumulate the support of the national convention delegates. This second competition is the one that legally determines the party's nomination. Both the national race and the delegate race are determined by the outcome of the primaries and caucuses.

As will be discussed more in Chapter 3, the election-year battle begins with the Iowa caucuses in early January or February. In Iowa, hearty souls tromp through the winter snow and ice to attend a weeknight neighborhood meeting. On the Democratic side, the candidate preferences of those who attend these neighborhood caucuses determine the selection of representatives to go on to higher level meetings, where delegates to the state and national conventions will be chosen. In the Republican caucuses, a straw poll is taken of candidate preferences, but these preferences are not directly tied to the selection of delegates. Turnout in these caucuses is small in terms of both absolute numbers and the percentage of the Iowa electorate. In 2008, the Iowa Democratic caucuses attracted 239,000 participants while 119,188 Republicans attended their caucuses. Iowa's voting age population in 2008 was 2,294,375, so the combined turnout at the caucuses was only 16 percent of the eligible electorate.[30] This turnout level is lower than most presidential primaries, though it is higher than any other caucus.

The real importance of the Iowa caucuses is for the national race, not the delegate race. The Iowa caucuses, and the New Hampshire primary, receive disproportionate amounts of media coverage. In fact, by some counts these initial events receive one-fourth or more of the total media coverage given to the primaries and caucuses.[31] Thus, the outcomes are magnified. An early victory can provide a candidate with momentum for the upcoming primaries, as happened with John Kerry in 2004. As Table 2.2 shows, four of the last five candidates (excluding Bush's renomination in 2004 from this count) claiming the ultimate nomination prize won the Iowa caucuses. The sole exception is John McCain in 2008, who averred he was not competing in them. On the Republican side, several leading candidates over the years have not competed in the Iowa caucuses. Thus, when McCain's early ventures into Iowa in 2007 did not pay off in increased support, he removed Iowa from his strategy and concentrated on the New Hampshire primary instead. The media tend not to fault candidates for doing poorly in an event if the candidate claims not to be campaigning in the state. However, if a candidate makes a state a key to his campaign, as Giuliani did with Florida in 2008, and then does not win this event, the media judgment will be harsh.

Winning the Iowa caucuses is hard work. Candidates need hundreds of volunteers to help them get their supporters to the caucuses. Campaign volunteers place phone calls, go door to door, and send e-mails to potential

Table 2.2 Primaries and caucuses won by nominees, 2000–2008

	Iowa	New Hampshire	Early schedule		Super Tuesday		Other competitive		Post-competitive		End date
			Primary	Caucus	Primary	Caucus	Primary	Caucus	Primary	Caucus	
2000											
Bush	Yes	No	4/6	2/2	6/10	2/2			25/25	1/1	March 9
Gore	Yes	Yes			11/11	4/4			25/25	8/8	March 9
2004											
Kerry	Yes	Yes	9/10	7/7	8/9	1/1			17/18	4/4	March 3
2008											
McCain	No	Yes	2/3	0/2	11/16	0/6	9/10	1/2	11/11	0/0	March 4
Obama	Yes	No	1/1	0/1	7/16	6/6	12/20	6/6			June 3

Sources: Rhodes Cook, "2000 Primary and Caucuses: Who Can Vote and How They Voted," http://www.rhodescook.com/analysis/presidential_primaries/national/natchart.html (accessed July 13, 2009); Rhodes Cook, "2004: The Voting Begins," http://www.rhodescook.com/primary.analysis.html (accessed July 13, 2009); and Norrander, "Democratic Marathon, Republican Sprint."

Note: Includes only U.S. states. 2000 Republican excludes New York primary, which was delegate vote only. Super Tuesday was March 7, 2000. 2004 Democrats excludes early Washington, DC primary which did not award delegates. Super Tuesday date was March 2, 2004. 2008 Democrats excludes Michigan and Florida primaries which were originally stripped of all delegates. Other competitive primaries for Republicans included those primaries after Super Tuesday still contested by Huckabee until McCain accumulated 50 percent of delegate total. Super Tuesday was February 5, 2008.

supporters urging them to participate in the caucuses. Candidates hold frequent campaign events in the weeks before Iowa. With not too much effort, an interested Iowan could attend a rally for Obama on one day and shake hands with Edwards on the next day. In the weeks before caucus night, Iowa's television and radio stations are saturated with candidate commercials. Money and organization are key to winning Iowa, but precise predictions of the outcome are impossible to devise. Who will actually attend, the distribution of candidates' supporters across 1,600 election precincts, and whether attendees will change their minds at the last minute all make caucus night tense for the candidates and their handlers.

The New Hampshire primary follows close on the heels of Iowa. In 2008, for the first time only five days separated the two events. New Hampshire is another state that receives the intense retail politics of numerous candidate visits. Media coverage is again intense. The electorate, however, is larger in a primary than a caucus. On the Democratic side, 287,557 voters participated in the 2008 New Hampshire primary and on the Republican side, another 239,328 voted, for a turnout rate of 51 percent. Still the number of New Hampshire voters is dwarfed by the four million voters participating in the Texas primary and the nearly eight million in California. Once again, it is not the size of the electorate or the number of delegates awarded that makes a victory in New Hampshire important. It is the media attention that such a victory garners.

Two of the last five presidential nominees failed to win the New Hampshire primary, so winning a party's nomination is possible without winning in New Hampshire. Yet, each of the eventual nominees won at least one of the first two contests. The last candidate to secure the presidential nomination and lose in both Iowa and New Hampshire was Bill Clinton in 1992. The Iowa caucuses were not crucial in that year because Iowa's Senator Tom Harkins was a candidate and dominated those contests.

With the Iowa and New Hampshire results, the attrition process begins in earnest. Those candidates who do poorly begin to drop out of the contest. Many of these candidates have simply run out of campaign resources. They often lagged behind in campaign funds to begin with and needed an early victory to refresh their campaign coffers. A prolonged campaign, without winning results, has other costs as well. Most of these candidates are career politicians who will need to work with the party in governance or in future campaigns. Prolonging an intraparty battle when it is unnecessary can hurt the reputations of these office-seeking politicians. Thus, they tend to leave the presidential nomination race quite quickly once their campaigns falter. As shown in Table 2.3, in almost every recent election contest, some candidates drop out immediately after the Iowa caucuses or New Hampshire primary.

Other candidates, however, do not drop out of the race as quickly. These candidates are better described as advocacy candidates. They have little

Table 2.3 The attrition game

Exit date	Candidate name	Candidate type	Period	Reason for exit
Rep: 2000				
1/26/2000	Orrin Hatch	Office seeking	Iowa/New Hampshire	Last in Iowa
2/4/2000	Gary Bauer	Advocacy	Iowa/New Hampshire	Placed fourth in Iowa, fifth in New Hampshire
2/9/2000	Steve Forbes	Office seeking	Other Early	Selected Delaware as key primary and then lost
3/9/2000	John McCain	Office seeking	Super Tuesday	After Super Tuesday too far behind in delegate totals
No formal exit	Alan Keyes	Advocacy	Post-Competitive	
Dem: 2000				
3/9/2000	Bill Bradley	Office seeking	Super Tuesday	After Super Tuesday had no primary victories
Dem: 2004				
1/19/2004	Dick Gephardt	Office seeking	Iowa/New Hampshire	Iowa loss
2/4/2004	Joe Lieberman	Office seeking	Other Early	No victories in early primaries
2/11/2004	Wesley Clark	Office seeking	Other Early	Won only one (Oklahoma) out of eight early primaries
2/18/2004	Howard Dean	Office seeking	Other Early	No victories in first nine primaries, left after losing Wisconsin primary
3/3/2004	John Edwards	Office seeking	Super Tuesday	Super Tuesday losses
3/15/2004	Al Sharpton	Advocacy	Post-Competitive	
7/22/2004	Dennis Kucinich	Advocacy	Post-Competitive	

Continued

Table 2.3 Cont'd

Exit date	Candidate name	Candidate type	Period	Reason for exit
Rep: 2008				
1/18/2008	Duncan Hunter	Advocacy	Iowa/New Hampshire	Poor vote totals
1/22/2008	Fred Thompson	Office seeking	Other Early	Selected South Carolina as key primary and then lost
1/30/2008	Rudy Giuliani	Office seeking	Other Early	Selected Florida as key primary and then lost
2/7/2008	Mitt Romney	Office seeking	Super Tuesday	Super Tuesday losses
3/4/2008	Mike Huckabee	Office seeking	Late Competitive	McCain had accumulated 50 percent of convention delegates
4/15/2008	Alan Keyes	Advocacy	Post-Competitive	Left Republican Party
6/12/2008	Ron Paul	Advocacy	Post-Competitive	
Dem: 2008				
1/4/2008	Joe Biden	Office Seeking	Iowa/New Hampshire	Loss in Iowa
1/4/2008	Christopher Dodd	Office Seeking	Iowa/New Hampshire	Loss in Iowa
1/10/2008	Bill Richardson	Office Seeking	Iowa/New Hampshire	Loss in New Hampshire
1/24/2008	Dennis Kucinich	Advocacy	Other Early	Left to defend House seat
1/30/2008	John Edwards	Office seeking	Other Early	No victory in first four contests
3/25/2008	Mike Gravel	Advocacy	Late Competitive	Left to pursue Libertarian Party nomination, which he also lost
6/7/2008	Hillary Clinton	Office seeking	Late Competitive	Last primary held, Obama held 50 percent of delegates

realistic chance of winning the nomination but are campaigning to high-light a particular political philosophy or to represent a core constituency group within the party. These advocacy candidates often are able to run low cost campaigns, relying on debate participation, campaign stops, and media coverage, rather than expensive campaign commercials, to promote their causes. Also since these advocacy candidates tend to come from positions other than high elective offices, they are less concerned about their reputation among other party elites. Thus, advocacy candidates often remain in the race, sometimes even after another candidate has attained the delegate total needed to secure the nomination.[32]

Every presidential nomination victory depends upon winning more than the Iowa caucuses and the New Hampshire primary. A second phase of the primary and caucus calendar includes a few more early events. The number of these contests and the number of days covered by these contests varies by election year. Frequently, candidates who failed to win in Iowa or New Hampshire will channel their resources into one of these contests hoping for a victory somewhere. Sometimes they fail to win the victory, as was the case for Forbes in 2000. In which case, the candidate exits the nomination contest during the other early primary phase. Even if a candidate wins one of these events, she or he may have spent so much time and resources on this contest that they are ill prepared to contest the multi-state Super Tuesday which follows.

By the time the nomination contest reaches Super Tuesday, the weaker candidates have been culled from the field. With the increasing front-loading of the presidential primary calendar, Super Tuesdays have become more frequent and larger. In 2008, nearly half the states chose February 5 for their primary or caucuses. Some commentators turned to calling it Super Duper Tuesday or Tsunami Tuesday to reflect its size. Returning to Table 2.2 shows that in three of the last five competitive nomination contests, the race, for all practical purposes, came to a close on Super Tuesday. In 2000, the early frontrunners of Bush and Gore bested McCain and Bradley, with Bush winning two-thirds of these contests and Gore all of them. Similarly in 2004 Kerry won 90 percent of the Super Tuesday contests, closing out the contest for that year. In all three cases, these candidates swept the remaining primaries and caucuses that occurred after Super Tuesday during the "post-competitive" period.[33] In 2008 McCain, while not winning in the caucuses, did win two-thirds of the Super Tuesday primaries. As Huckabee remained in the contest after Super Tuesday, a short "other competitive" primary period occurred. Yet, McCain won almost all of the events during this period, and Huckabee dropped out in early March, leaving McCain to sweep the "post-competitive" primaries. Only the 2008 Democratic contest remained competitive throughout the full primary and caucus calendar, as Obama and Clinton split primary results on Super Tuesday and in the "other competitive" primary stage.

The multi-state victories by these candidates on Super Tuesday set into motion the delegate accumulation contest. The Super Tuesday contests are numerous and include some of the largest states with the most delegates at stake. A candidate who wins on Super Tuesday adds a large number of delegates to his or her column. After Super Tuesday, most of the other candidates lag behind the frontrunner. The gap in the delegate totals is now enough to convince most of the remaining serious presidential contenders to leave the contest. In fact, a delegate lead equal to 25–30 percent of the delegate total needed for nomination is often sufficient to convince the remaining office-seeking candidates to leave the field. Thus, in four of the five competitive nomination races we have examined, for all practical purposes, the race came to a close immediately after Super Tuesday. In 2000, McCain and Bradley drop out; in 2004, John Edwards bows out; and in 2008, Romney exits the race. Mike Huckabee did not concede the 2008 Republican race to McCain immediately after Super Tuesday. Yet, McCain soundly defeated Huckabee in the next round of primaries and by March 4 had won the needed 50 percent of the convention delegates. The top portion of Figure 2.3 shows how McCain continually added to his delegate totals, while Romney and then Huckabee fell far behind before dropping out of the nomination contest. In five of the six nomination contests since 2000, Super Tuesday results gave one candidate a sizable lead in convention delegates and most of the remaining contestants soon bowed out.

The sole exception in the last three election cycles was the 2008 Democratic contest, and the bottom portion of Figure 2.3 shows how Clinton's and Obama's delegate totals kept pace with one another throughout the campaign. Hillary Clinton had planned her campaign strategy around a dramatic Super Tuesday victory that would lead the remaining candidates to leave the contests. After all, this was the pattern of recent years. But she and Obama split the primaries on Super Tuesday and Obama won the caucuses. Coming out of Super Duper Tuesday, Clinton and Obama had almost identical totals among the pledged delegates allocated according to electoral contests results: 625 for Clinton, 624 for Obama. Clinton still had greater support among the unpledged superdelegates, composed of the party elite such as members of Congress and high party officials. Thus Clinton led in total delegates: 818 to 730. Yet, one or the other candidate would still need to win more than 1,200 additional delegates to garner the support of the 50 percent of the Democratic delegates needed to secure the nomination.[34]

Obama's strategy of contesting the caucuses and being prepared for the post-Super Tuesday contests gave him momentum in the second half of February. He took the delegate lead on February 12, but only by a margin of 42 delegates. Momentum shifted back to Clinton with important primary victories in early March in Ohio and Texas. With so many of the

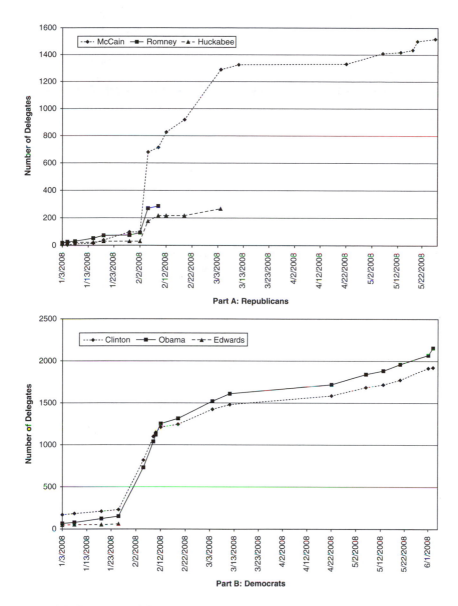

Figure 2.3 Convention delegate totals, 2008.
Source: Delegate totals from CNN webpages.

primaries scheduled for the front of the primary calendar, no state held a primary between March 12 and April 21. A three-week campaign led to another Clinton victory in Pennsylvania. The two candidates split the remaining primaries. At the close of the last primaries on June 3, Obama led Clinton in delegates by only 233 delegates: 2,156 for Obama and 1,923 for Clinton. Yet, Obama had surpassed the magic number of 2,118 delegates needed to win the nomination. The 2008 Democratic contest lasted to the last round of primaries because neither Obama nor Clinton was able to draw sufficiently ahead in the delegate count to convince the other to withdraw.

Obama won only one more primary than Clinton in 2008, but he won all but one of the 14 caucus states.[35] Other than the Iowa caucuses, most candidates ignore the caucus states. Turnout is low and hard to predict. Television advertising dollars are better spent in primary states where more actual voters will see them. Caucus states require a lot of grassroots mobilization. In 2008, however, two candidates did pay attention to these caucuses, with different results. The delegates Obama won in the caucus states helped him put together the narrow delegate margin that won him the nomination. Romney on the Republican side also spent time and money in the caucus states and he won most of these. Romney, however, failed to put together a convincing string of primary victories. He won only three, and all were "home states." Romney won in Massachusetts, where he had been governor; in Michigan, where his father had been governor; and in Utah, with its many Mormon voters. Candidates are expected to win in such states, and so do not receive much credit from the media when they do so.

The presidential nominations for the Democratic and Republican parties are won through a two-tiered system. At one level, candidates compete for public support in a national race, where primary and caucus results serve to bolster the fortunes of some candidates and lead others to withdraw. At the second level, convention delegates are allocated to the presidential candidates based on the results of the primaries and caucuses. When one candidate can claim the support of 50 percent of these convention delegates, that candidate will be assured of being formally nominated for president at the party's national convention. Yet in many cases, even before one candidate secures 50 percent of the delegates, most of the other candidates have withdrawn.

Changing Technology, Changing Campaign Strategies

The way that candidates campaign for the presidential nominations is affected as much by changes in technology as by the rules created by the parties and the dates chosen by the states for their primaries or caucuses.

Each new technology is incorporated into candidates' strategies. In the 1930s, Franklin Delano Roosevelt distributed phonographic records to potential supporters, as well as writing letters and placing telephone calls.[36] Reliable and more available airline travel after World War II allowed Harold Stassen to crisscross the country in an early attempt to center a nomination bid on primary victories. In the 1970s, campaign consultants began to develop the lists of names that would be the basis for direct mail campaigns. These consultants would send out hundreds of thousands of letters in hope that a small percentage of recipients would return a campaign contribution averaging $25. Increasingly these consultants were able to hone the list of names to be able to send potential donors tailor-made appeals based on interest in specific issues or causes. Direct mail fundraising tended to work better for more ideological candidates and for contacting older Americans. In the 1980s, candidates sent out videotape cassettes to potential donors and likely voters in key contests. During his 1992 presidential bid, Jerry Brown frequently recited his 1-800 toll-free telephone number to solicit campaign contributions.[37]

The internet is increasingly used to obtain small campaign donations. John McCain in 2000 was the first to successfully employ this technique. The internet has a number of advantages over previous methods for soliciting small campaign contributions. Foremost, candidates do not have to identify potential donors in advance, as they did with direct mail. Fundraising on the internet is inexpensive and results can be quick. Further, candidates' webpages do more than solicit contributions. These webpages provide a wealth of information about a candidate's background and issue positions. Vignettes of supporters can convince others with similar characteristics to make contributions. Sites include video clips of speeches, retransmissions of television commercials, and made-for-the-internet videos to get the candidate's message out to the American public.

The internet will not replace traditional forms of fundraising. Candidates will still seek out wealthy individuals who can solicit their networks of friends, business associates and acquaintances for campaign contributions. Individual donors can give only a bit more than $2,000 as their individual contribution to a candidate, but they can bundle together ten, twenty, or thirty $2,000 contributions from their friends and associates, as well. In addition, candidates will continue to raise funds by holding $2,000-a-plate dinners or $500 per person cocktail parties.

New technology is used for more than raising campaign funds. In 2004, Howard Dean used the internet to recruit volunteers and facilitate communications among supporters. Followers were encouraged to join chat rooms, to write blogs and create webpages in support of Dean, and to use facilities such as Meetup.com to organize their own campaign events. By 2008, social networking sites such as Facebook and MySpace took center stage. Candidates had their own sites on these networks, with the public being granted automatic listings as supporters. Facebook would even report running tallies of the number of supporters for each candidate. At times, candidates may even lose control over their messages and images on the internet. Anyone can create webpages, blogs, or Facebook groups in support of or opposition to a candidate. Anyone can upload a video to YouTube. E-mail chains pass along fact and fiction about candidates and their positions.[38] The internet is a two-edged sword for the candidates. It allows them direct access to the public for fundraising and conveying their campaign messages. The internet, however, allows anyone to present her or his own interpretation of the candidates, including images that the candidates may not like.

Today candidates use a combination of new, old, and improved technology to reach out to voters, activists, and contributors. Candidates hire consultants who specialize in conducting public opinion polls and holding focus group sessions. Other consultants shape a candidate's advertisements using the latest knowledge on effective communications whether it be for broadcasting on television, airing on radio, or streaming over the internet. Public speeches and rallies are staged. Store-front headquarters are established in states with upcoming primaries or caucuses to recruit and organize the activities of local volunteers. Candidates are well prepped for candidate debates and important media interviews. Modern political campaigns are multifaceted and ever-evolving organizations.

Third-Party Nominations

Every year the general election ballots listing the contenders for the U.S. presidency contain more names than those of the Democratic and Republican candidates. In recent years, the Green Party, the Libertarian Party, and the Reform Party, among a host of other minor parties, have their candidates' names listed on at least some of the 50 states' presidential ballots. Most of these candidates are nominated by a convention.

A basic tension within these minor parties is the pull between wanting to nominate a candidate with broader name recognition who can draw in new votes for the party versus wanting a candidate who is more strictly in line with the party's issues. One of the best examples of a minor party nominating a more recognized name is the Green Party's selection of consumer advocate Ralph Nader as its presidential nominee in 1996 and 2000. In the latter year, Nader won 2.7 percent of the popular vote, and some felt that Nader cost Al Gore votes in key states. In 2008, both the Libertarian Party and the Green Party selected candidates who had formerly served in Congress as a member of one of the two major parties. The Libertarian Party nominated former Republican Georgia congressman Bob Barr on the sixth ballot. Those who opposed Barr felt that he did not sufficiently represent the party's positions on all the issues. In a less contentious convention, the Green Party nominated another former Georgia representative, former Democrat Cynthia McKinney.[39]

The Reform Party, which spun off from Ross Perot's two self-financed runs for the presidency in 1992 and 1996, experienced a particularly divisive convention in 2000. The candidate who won the nomination would be entitled to $12.6 million in campaign funds from the federal government due to the number of votes Perot had accumulated in 1996. (The Democratic and Republican party candidates in 2000 each received $67.6 million for their fall campaigns.) The Reform Party held a mail-in primary in July followed by a convention in August. Political commentator Pat Buchanan, who formerly ran for the Republican nomination in 1992 and 1996, vied off against John Hagelin, who had been the Natural Law Party candidate in 1992 and 1996. Buchanan supporters felt he would bring new energy to the party, while his detractors feared Buchanan would put too much emphasis on social conservatism. The Reform Party convention broke down into factions. When Buchanan won the nomination, Hagelin and his supporters broke with the party and eventually merged back in with the Natural Law Party. Buchanan and the Reform Party won .4 percent of the fall presidential election vote, and Hagelin .08 percent.[40]

Nomination Controversies

The three cycles of presidential nominations at the start of the 21st century produced candidates for the Democratic and Republican parties that were both typical and atypical. In electoral background, they all shared the experience of serving as a governor or senator. Their personal backgrounds were more rich and diverse. Yet each was nominated under the same system of contesting primaries and caucuses across the 50 states (and a few territories) to win the support of the party's national convention delegates. Each also was competing to win the support of the American public. While at least one of these pairs of candidates would have to lose in the fall general election, all six nominees received a substantial portion of the presidential vote. None lost in a landslide, and each won the support of approximately 90 percent of their own party's voters. The primary-dominated system produced candidates acceptable to a large majority of their party's voters.

Yet, the primary-dominated nomination system has its critics, and various controversies arise in each nomination cycle. The close race in 2008 between Obama and Clinton provoked disagreements over how to handle states that did not conform to national rules in scheduling their primaries. As the race lasted into April and June questions began to arise on whether the party's delegate allocation rules were needlessly prolonging the battle. On the other hand, Republican voters in Pennsylvania, North Carolina, and Oregon did not have much say in the 2008 nomination, as

McCain had secured enough delegates to be the presumptive nominee before their states voted. Finally, what does it mean that the strongest candidates abandoned the federal campaign matching funds system that had shaped nomination politics since the 1970s? In the next chapter, we will examine the criticisms often lodged at the primary-dominated nomination system.

Chapter 3

Is This a Fair Way to Select a Presidential Nominee?

The long, neck-and-neck battle in 2008 between Barack Obama and Hillary Clinton for the Democratic nomination brought to the surface many old questions about the effects and fairness of various sets of rules. Did the Democratic Party's use of proportional representation rules needlessly prolong the battle between the two candidates by making it more difficult to win a large majority of the delegates from any state? Were the caucuses fair with their limited participation levels? Would the Democratic Party's superdelegates swing the outcome in a different direction than the public vote? Meanwhile, McCain's quicker victory on the Republican side led to fewer criticisms on the Republican side. Yet, Republican rules translated McCain's primary victories into a larger delegate lead. Election rules matter, and U.S. presidential nomination politics has lots of rules.

As we saw in the first two chapters, many different forces shape the conduct of presidential nomination politics. Some of these factors are party rules, such as the Democratic Party rules requiring proportional representation or creating superdelegates. Yet, the structure of the nomination calendar is mostly determined by the actions of state legislatures or state parties. State laws also have the most to say about which voters can participate, though the national Democratic Party has some rules on this as well. Some of the criticism of the nomination system is not with the parties and their rules, but with other players. For example, concerns are often expressed over media bias. Was the coverage of Barack Obama in 2008 and John McCain in 2000 too friendly? Do the media give too much attention to Iowa and New Hampshire? In addition, others question whether activists and campaign donors push candidates to more ideologically extreme positions.

Criticisms of the presidential nomination system ebb and flow. Some of this is part of the reform cycle. A new set of reforms is followed by a period where some additional refinements are needed to overcome unexpected outcomes or further work out the specifics of the reform. Thus, the Democratic Party throughout much of the 1980s continued to adjust their party rules. Specific contests also bring up questions of fairness or effects. Thus, the long battle in 1984 between Walter Mondale and Gary Hart posed many of the same concerns as the Democratic battle in 2008. "Did the superdelegates help out Mondale?" was as frequent a question in 1984 as "Will the superdelegates help Clinton?" was in 2008. In the intervening years, when the outcome of the nomination was determined more quickly, fewer debates emerged over the rules. A strong front-runner will win under most any set of participation, delegate allocation, or calendar rules.

The American public has mixed feelings about the presidential nomination process. About half the public, in response to public opinion polls, agree that the current system does indeed nominate the best qualified candidate. Yet, many feel that they do not learn enough about the candidates during the primary season. They complain that not enough attention is paid to the issues and that they do not learn about the candidates' trustworthiness and ability to govern the country. Many also feel that the media and money have too much influence on the outcome. Finally, a majority are unhappy that Iowa and New Hampshire always start out the nomination election calendar.[1]

In this chapter, a host of criticisms about the current nomination process will be explored. We will begin with the general criticisms asserting that the overall process is flawed. One of these arguments is that winning the nominations has become an endurance contest that does not test the skills needed for being an effective president. Candidates begin their quests for the presidency two or three years in advance in order to garner sufficient resources during the invisible primary stage. Other arguments proclaim that the primary process contributes to the polarization of the political parties where the Republican Party has moved to the right and the Democratic Party to the left. Such polarized parties make bipartisan alliances in government more difficult to achieve. Finally, primaries are viewed as potentially divisive within each party. Supporters of losing candidates may not be willing to back the party's nominee in the fall election.

Some of the criticisms about the primary-centered nomination process focus on specific rules. Rules determine the ability of voters to participate in the nomination process. One set of rules places restrictions on who can vote in the primaries. Some primaries are closed, allowing only their own party members to vote. Some primaries are open, allowing anyone to vote. Some primaries fall in between, allowing only independents the option to vote in either party's primary. A second concern focusing on voter participation is renewed questions over whether the caucus format is fair, given the low numbers of participants and a single meeting time. Another set of rules concerns the delegates selected through the primary process. Are the rules that distribute the delegate totals to the states fair? What about the rules which allocate delegates to candidates based on the outcomes of the primary elections? Finally, should party officials and elected officials, such as senators and governors, be automatically represented at the party's convention? And should these unelected delegates be free to back any of the candidates?

The most frequent criticism of the primary-centered nomination process in recent years is that the calendar of primaries and caucuses has become too front-loaded. More and more states are trying to hold their primaries or caucuses as early as possible on the election calendar. In 2008, this culminated in nearly half of the states holding their primaries on February 5, the first date available to most states. Front-loading, however, can be traced back to the 1980s. Many critics are concerned that front-loading puts too much of a premium on fundraising, advantages early frontrunners, and does not give voters sufficient time to learn about the candidates. Such criticisms over front-loading often lead into advocacy for calendar reforms, such as regional primaries or a single national primary.

General Criticisms of Primary-Centered Nominations

Some critics argue the entire process of nominating candidates by presidential primaries and caucuses is fundamentally flawed. They assert that this nomination process tests the endurance of candidates but not their presidential skills. Candidates must spend a year, or two or three, traveling around the country to build up name recognition, cultivate support among party activists, and raise campaign funds. These critics aver that candidates must make narrow issue appeals to attract early support from activists and donors who may be more ideologically extreme than the average American voter. Further, candidates are not screened for their competence in governing, their abilities to work with Congress or foreign leaders, or their skills at building the coalitions within and across parties that will be necessary for passing legislation.[2]

Many of these criticisms first arose in reaction to the nominations of George McGovern in 1972 and Jimmy Carter in 1976. McGovern was viewed as a candidate too extreme to win the presidency, and Carter, while winning the presidency, as someone ill prepared for the nitty-gritty politics of Washington, DC. Yet, McGovern and Carter won their nominations in the first two election cycles of the new primary-dominated nomination process before more established candidates understood the new dynamics. By 1980, all the major candidates knew the new rules: run in all the primaries and win early and often. Presidential nominees since 1980 have been candidates who demonstrated wide popular appeal before, during, and after the primaries. These candidates often led in the national polls prior to the first primary and accumulated early endorsements from other senators and governors. They secured their nominations with numerous victories in the presidential primaries. In general, the parties' voters seemed pleased with these nomination choices. Between 1980 and 2008, on average 84 percent of Democrats and 86 percent of Republicans (and independents who lean toward each party) voted for their party's presidential candidate in the fall election.[3]

Qualities of Primary Voters

Another general criticism of primaries is that the primary electorate is too ideological. By this, critics mean that Democratic primary voters are too much on the liberal end of the spectrum and Republican primary voters are too much on the conservative end. In contrast, general election voters are viewed as more moderate. Primary elections are said to be a centrifugal force in U.S. politics, pulling the parties away from the voters in the middle of the ideological array. This leads to a polarization of the parties, so that in Congress the Democratic members are at one end of the ideological spectrum and the Republicans at the other end.

Primaries have lower turnout rates than do general elections, but does this distort the composition of the primary electorate? Turnout in some primary elections can be very low, but this is more common for congressional primaries than for presidential primaries. Calculating turnout rates in primaries is a bit more complex than doing so for general elections. Since primaries are partisan events, the normal base for calculating turnout in the United States (i.e., the size of the voting age population in each state) needs to be divided between those with generalized Republican versus Democratic leanings. State partisanship figures can be ascertained from public opinion polls and these values can be used to subdivide a state's potential voters into two partisan groups.[4] The result of this division will be termed the partisan voting age population, with one for the Republican Party and one for the Democratic Party. Using these measures of turnout, participation in the 2008 Republican presidential primaries averaged 21 percent of the partisan voting age population, while turnout in Democratic primaries averaged 35 percent of the partisan voting age population. In the November 2008 general election, the turnout level was 57 percent.[5] Averaging turnout rates in the Democratic and Republican primaries suggests that turnout in the primaries is about half of that in the fall general election. The earliest study of presidential primaries from 1916 to 1924 also found turnout in presidential primaries to be one-quarter to one-half that of the subsequent general election.[6] Thus, turnout in presidential primaries is smaller than in the fall general election, but not so small that the electorate necessarily is a distortion of more general preferences in the state.

Turnout levels in presidential primaries reflect the amount of interest in the contest. A close, exciting race draws out more voters. Thus, in 2008, higher turnouts were found on the Democratic rather than Republican side. The amount of campaign spending also matters. More dollars spent means more commercials, more campaign rallies, and more local offices set up to recruit volunteers. With record spending by Clinton and Obama in 2008, primary participation also was high. Yet, this is not a new pattern. Studies by scholars from the 1920s, 1970s, and 1980s demonstrated that the more money spent and the closer the contest, the higher the primary turnout.[7] Give the American public an interesting contest and they will come out to the polls, even if it is a primary election.

Exactly who turns out to vote in the presidential primaries? In most years, the presidential primary electorate is composed of those who are slightly older, slightly more partisan, more interested in politics, and more aware of the candidates and the issues. Most scholarly studies find few differences between presidential primary voters and nonvoting members of their party on issues positions or candidate preferences. Nor are presidential primary voters distinctive in their ideological positions. Rather than being a more ideologically extreme proportion of the electorate, presidential primary voters are more aptly described as the slightly more interested and knowledgeable segment of the electorate.[8]

If the presidential primary voters are not pulling the parties' candidates outward, who is? Some scholars and journalists argue it is the activists and donors that pull candidates to the extremes.[9] Party activists and donors care about specific issues and, unlike most Americans, activists pay attention to the candidates during the invisible primary stage. These activists may be liberals demanding an end to a war or greater protection of the environment. They may be conservative activists concerned about taxes on small businesses or new restrictions on gun ownership. Candidates make promises to these activists and donors in order to raise money to compete effectively for the support of the voters in the subsequent visible primaries.

Are Primaries Divisive?

One of the earliest criticisms of presidential primaries, and primaries in general, is that they could divide the political party into two camps: those who supported the candidate who won the nomination and those who supported another candidate. If those who supported one of the losing candidates held intense feelings, they may be unwilling to support the party's nominee in the fall election. In other words, the primaries could become divisive. The 1912 Republican nomination battle between Taft and Roosevelt certainly seemed to confirm this thesis. Nelson Polsby, a political scientist critical of primary elections, argued that primaries are inherently divisive because they lead candidates to cater to specific party factions rather than building broader-based coalitions.[10]

Whether primaries are divisive depends upon a number of factors. Divisive primaries might actually be a symptom rather than a cause of party dissension. A sitting president would be more likely to be seriously challenged for renomination if the president were unpopular with a segment of the party's core constituency. Likewise, if a party was divided over a significant issue, the outcome of the primaries may appear to be divisive as one candidate is supported by party members on one side of this issue and a second candidate is supported by party members on the other side of the issue. Which candidate lost out in a nomination contest may also matter. If a more moderate candidate lost to a more ideologically extreme candidate, the supporters of the losing candidate might be more likely to defect to the opposition party's candidate. If the more ideologically extreme candidate lost to a more moderate candidate, the supporters of the extreme candidate would not have much in common with the opposition party's candidate. They would, by necessity, become reluctant supporters of their own party's candidate.

The 2008 battle between Senators Clinton and Obama renewed concerns over the divisive primary thesis. It was the first long battle for a party's nomination since the 1980s. Both candidates had ardent supporters. Would those primary voters who cast their ballots for Clinton be less likely to vote for Obama in the fall campaign? What about the party activists who had worked hard in hopes of seeing the first female presidential nominee from a major political party? Yet, the battle between Clinton and Obama ended at the beginning of June with the last round of primary votes. Clinton endorsed Obama when she withdrew from the race in June and again in August at the national convention.

Clinton's supporters did move to support Obama. Gallup poll results show Clinton's endorsement of Obama at the convention increased support for Obama. Before the convention, 70 percent of former Clinton supporters were willing to vote for Obama; after the convention the number rose to 81 percent.[11] According to the media exit polls, 83 percent of Democrats who had supported Clinton in the primaries voted for Obama in the November general election. Furthermore, the Obama and Clinton primary campaigns mobilized many new voters and activists. Those who had talked or e-mailed their friends to support Obama in the primaries or made an on-line contribution were likely to continue this activity for the fall campaign, as well. Intense primary campaigns mobilize new groups of supporters, which can benefit the party in the fall election.[12]

Presidential primaries have always had their critics and their supporters. No one expects that the parties will turn away from the primaries. The American public has grown accustomed to having a voice in the parties' presidential nominations. Yet, many specific elements of the current nomination process can be questioned and possibly changed. Some rules govern the ability of citizens to participate in the nomination process.

Participation in primaries may be limited to registered partisans or open to all. The caucus structure places a greater burden on those wishing to participate. The legal function of the primaries and caucuses is to select convention delegates. How fair are the rules that apportion these delegates across the states and those that distribute each state's delegates to the candidates? Finally, many of the concerns in recent years are a reaction to an election calendar that has become increasingly front-loaded. Iowa and New Hampshire lead off the election-year event, but soon after, an onslaught of primaries and caucuses are clumped together as other states also want a decisive say in the presidential nominations. It is this last set of concerns that has led to many calls for reforms, grouping states by geography or population size, or scrapping the sequential state-by-state series of primaries for a single national primary. These reforms will be the topic of Chapter 4. First, potential biases, or strengths, of the current rules will be explored, beginning with the rules for voter participation.

Who Should Vote

Primaries are the mechanism by which the parties select their nominees. Thus, some feel that it is best for the parties to be able to limit participation in the primaries to those who are willing to call themselves a member of the party. This would let party members choose the candidate that best reflects the preferences of the party's voters. A closed primary requires that those who wish to vote in the Republican Party declare themselves as a Republican when they register to vote. Likewise, for the Democratic primary. Independents cannot vote in a closed primary state, but fewer citizens register as independents in closed primary states.[13] Closed primaries help a party build a consistent base of supporters in the electorate, and the requirement of having to register as either a Democrat or a Republican to participate is hardly onerous. Further, the U.S. Supreme Court has consistently supported the political parties' right to limit the participation in their primaries to their own partisans, or to any other combination that the party may wish to include.[14] These Supreme Court rulings are based on the parties' First Amendment rights of association. Opponents of closed primaries argue that all voters should be able to participate in the primaries. Critics also argue that the electorate in a closed primary state becomes too polarized, with the Democratic electorate being composed of mostly liberals and the Republican electorate being mostly conservatives. As such, the winning candidates are viewed as more extreme.

In open primary states, voter registration forms do not ask for party affiliation. Voters on election day choose in which party's primary they wish to vote. In some open primary states, voters must tell the poll officials which party's ballot they wish to receive. In other open primary states, voters receive both parties' ballots (or both are listed on the same ballot), but voters can only select candidates from a single party. Proponents of open primaries view them as providing a greater opportunity for participation for all voters. Some party leaders also may view open primaries as a way to attract more voters to their party.

Critics of the open primary format fear that one party's supporters may "raid" the primary of the other party. These "crossover" voters may vote for the weakest candidate in the opposite party's primary. The strategy of raiding voters is to give their own party's candidate an edge in the fall general election by ensuring that the opposition party nominates a weaker competitor. Little evidence exists of raiding in open primaries. People who cross over and vote in the opposition party's primary do so to cast a ballot for a preferred candidate. Rather than trying to weaken the other party's nominee, crossover voters are trying to ensure that they have two acceptable candidates to choose from in the fall election. Still, the preferences of the crossover voters may be different from those of party voters. One such example occurred in 2000, when the Republican Party in Michigan held an early primary on a different date than the Democratic primary. Such a situation allowed for more Democrats to cross over and vote in the Republican primary. John McCain won the Michigan primary in 2000 on the basis of votes from Democrats and independents, while two-thirds of the Republicans voted for George W. Bush.[15]

In between open and closed primaries are semi-open primaries. In these states, those registered as a Democrat or Republican are restricted to their own party's primary. Those who register as independents, however, are able to choose on election day in which party's primary they would like to participate. In these states, many more voters register as independents. The exact rules vary by state, but in New Hampshire voters registered as "undeclared" can request either party's ballot at the primary election. Voting in a party's primary enrolls the voter in that party, but these New Hampshire voters can return to their undeclared status by filling out a card before leaving the polling place. Semi-open primary rules do prevent opposite party partisans from voting in a primary. On the other hand, the semi-open primary rule produces the highest number of independent voters. In 2008, 31 percent of New Hampshire voters were registered as Democrats, 31 percent as Republicans, and 38 percent as undeclared. While potentially undeclared voters could swamp the partisan voters on either side of the New Hampshire ballot, 54 percent of the Democratic primary electorate professed a Democratic identification and 61 percent of the Republican electorate were Republicans.[16]

Does it matter whether a state holds a closed, open, or semi-open presidential primary? One effect could be to influence the level of participation, e.g., the turnout level. A common assumption is that open primaries should have higher turnout rates than closed primaries. Yet, no consistent empirical evidence backs up this assumption. Why? One reason is that voters do not deliberately disenfranchise themselves. In closed primary states, proportionately more voters register as Democrats or Republicans and fewer register as independents. A second reason open primaries do not increase turnout is because the circumstances in which a large number of people would flock to one party's primary over the other are rare. If both parties have competitive primaries, most voters will stick with the primary of their preferred party. Neither party's primary will have unusually high turnout. Only in an instance when one party's primary remains competitive while the other party's is not would there be incentive for many voters to cross over into the other party's primary and increase the turnout rate. Yet, this is more likely to happen near the close of the primary schedule, and many of the later primaries coincided with the state's primaries for other offices. Thus, even if the presidential nomination battle has ended for one party, primary contests for other offices may keep the party's voters in their own party's primary.

The Democratic contest in 2008, however, is one example where Republicans (and independents) may have had an incentive to cross over to vote in the later Democratic primaries. The Republican race concluded in many ways after Super Tuesday when Romney bowed out of the race. Huckabee continued to vie against McCain until March 4, so for some Republican voters only after March 4 would they have an incentive to vote on the Democratic ballot. The long pause in the 2008 primary schedule before the Pennsylvania primary on April 22 did produce reports of voters reregistering in order to participate in the Democratic primary on that date.

In general, turnout was higher in the Democratic than the Republican primaries in 2008. On average, using the partisan proportions of the voting age population, turnout in the Democratic primaries averaged 35 percent and turnout in Republican primaries averaged 21 percent. Comparing turnout within each state, Democratic primary turnout tended to outpace Republican participation rates by 14 percentage points. The relative competitiveness of the two party presidential contests mattered. Through Super Tuesday when both parties had competitive races, Democratic turnout exceeded Republican turnout on average by 6 percentage points. When the Republican race narrowed to Huckabee versus McCain, Democratic turnout exceeded Republican turnout on average by 22 percentage points. In the final phase, after Huckabee's withdrawal and McCain holding 50 percent of the delegate support, Democratic primary turnout exceeded Republican primary turnout by 27 percentage points.

The biggest differences in Democratic versus Republican primary turnout occurred after Super Tuesday and Romney's withdrawal from the Republican race. After this point, did the rules matter? One rule was the presence of a congressional primary held jointly with the presidential primaries.

This rule does not seem to have mattered. In the late primaries (after Super Tuesday) Democratic primary turnout exceeded Republican turnout by 23 percentage points if no congressional primary was held and by 25 percentage points if a congressional primary was held. There is no significant difference between these two values. What mattered were the participation rules. In the seven late primaries with closed primary rules, Democratic turnout exceeded Republican primary turnout by 18 percentage points. In the nine late primaries with open primary rules, the differences in turnout were 30 percentage points. The American voter in 2008 did take advantage of the open and semi-open primaries to vote in the more exciting Democratic race after McCain had apparently secured the Republican nomination.

How did the participation of independents and possibly Republican voters affect the outcome of the Democratic primaries held after Super Tuesday? Table 3.1 shows the actual vote for Clinton and Obama in these primaries in the leftmost columns of the table. From the exit polls taken at the time of the primaries, the vote of only those who identified themselves as Democrats is listed in the middle columns of the table. The final two columns subtract the actual vote from the vote by Democrats. These differences give the gains or losses for Clinton and Obama if only Democrats had been allowed to vote. Primaries are grouped together based on closed, open, or semi-open participation formats.

The values for the gains and losses for Clinton and Obama are quite small, averaging at 2.5 percentage points or less. In general, Clinton would have gained a few points in the overall vote if only Democrats had been allowed to vote and Obama would typically lose a few points. In no instance would restricting the electorate solely to Democratic adherents have changed the winning candidate for any primary. In the closed primaries, 81 percent of the electorate was composed of those who identified themselves as Democrats. The remaining participants professed an independent identification, though they were legally registered as Democrats. Obama did better than Clinton with these legally registered Democrats who still considered themselves to be independents. Since younger people often are more likely to view themselves as independents, this may be the underlying cause for the pattern in the closed primary states. In the three semi-open primaries, 73 percent of the electorate was composed of Democratic identifiers. Most of the other voters (on average 23 percent) viewed themselves as independent, since those registered as Republicans were excluded from the semi-open Democratic primary. Once again, Obama did slightly better with the independent voters, except in North Carolina where the pattern was reversed. In North Carolina, a large proportion of Democratic identifiers tended to be African Americans. Finally, in the open primary states, Democratic identifiers made up 65 percent of the Democratic primary electorate. Even though

Table 3.1 Changes in support for Clinton and Obama if only Democrats voted in primaries after Super Tuesday, by primary type

State	Date	Actual vote		Democratic vote		% Dem.	Gain only Dem.	
		Clinton	Obama	Clinton	Obama	Voters	Clinton	Obama
		Closed primaries						
LA	9-Feb	35.6	57.4	38.0	57.0	83.0	2.4	−0.4
MD	12-Feb	36.2	61.4	40.0	59.0	84.0	3.8	−2.4
PA	22-Apr	54.6	45.4	56.0	44.0	82.0	1.4	−1.4
KY	20-May	65.5	29.9	68.0	30.0	84.0	2.5	0.1
OR	20-May	40.5	58.5	45.0	55.0	71.0	4.5	−3.5
SD	3-Jun	55.3	44.7	56.0	44.0	83.0	0.7	−0.7
Average						81.2	2.5	−1.4
		Open primaries						
VA	12-Feb	35.5	63.7	38.0	62.0	70.0	2.5	−1.7
WI	19-Feb	40.8	58.1	46.0	53.0	62.0	5.2	−5.1
OH	4-Mar	53.5	44.8	56.0	42.0	69.0	2.5	−2.8
TX	4-Mar	51.4	47.8	53.0	46.0	66.0	1.6	−1.8
VT	4-Mar	38.6	59.3	40.0	57.0	55.0	1.4	−2.3
MS	11-Mar	36.7	61.2	30.0	67.0	71.0	−6.7	5.8
IN	6-May	50.6	49.4	52.0	48.0	67.0	1.4	−1.4
MT	3-Jun	41.1	56.6	43.0	55.0	60.0	1.9	−1.6
Average						65.0	1.2	−1.4
		Semi-open primaries						
RI	4-Mar	58.4	40.4	62.0	37.0	64.0	3.6	−3.4
NC	6-May	41.6	56.1	39.0	60.0	76.0	−2.6	3.9
WV	13-May	66.9	25.8	71.0	24.0	78.0	4.1	−1.8
Average						72.7	1.7	−0.4

Source: Official votes and votes by Democrats according to exit polls.

Republicans could vote in these open Democratic primaries, on average only 9 percent of these primary voters were Republicans. Once again, crossover voters were mostly independents. And once again, the presence of independents and a small number of Republican voters only altered the outcome by less than 2.5 percentage points. Turnout rose in the open and semi-open Democratic primaries after McCain had secured the nomination, but it was mostly independents (and perhaps more Democrats) who participated in these primaries.

Are Caucuses Fair?

Turnout in caucuses is very, very low. In 2008, participation rates in the caucuses averaged 4 percent for Republicans and 9 percent for Democrats.

Recall that turnout averaged 21 percent in Republican and 35 percent in Democratic primaries. One reason caucus turnout rates are so low is the requirement that everyone meet at the same time for a local meeting that may last several hours. In primary elections, voters often have 12 or more hours in which to arrive at the polling place, and some may vote by absentee ballots. Many people are unwilling to attend a meeting for several hours in order to express their preference for their party's presidential nomination. Others cannot attend due to other obligations at the designated times, such as work schedules or child care issues. The caucus format often requires individuals to take a public stance for their candidate. Individuals raise their hands or congregate in one section of the meeting room to designate their candidate preference. Some Americans may feel that this violates the secret ballot norms and be reluctant to participate.[17]

Defenders of the caucus format describe it as grassroots democracy. People from the neighborhood come together to meet and discuss the merits of the various presidential contenders. At some caucuses, participants also may be involved in discussions on issues for the state party's platform. Further, caucuses can be a mechanism for local parties to recruit new volunteers to help staff the local party organizations. The ideal of a give-and-take grassroots democracy, however, may not be met. William Mayer described a series of caucuses that he observed as "less an opportunity for citizens to 'come and reason together' than an occasion in which candidate enthusiasts come together to be counted."[18]

Besides criticisms of caucuses for low participation levels, additional concerns are expressed about the characteristics of those who do participate. Indeed, caucus attendees are more likely than primary voters to be demographically unrepresentative. Caucus attendees are better educated and wealthier. Some critics also view caucus participants as more ideologically extreme. Survey evidence shows Democratic participants to be liberals and Republican attendees to be conservative though neither group tends to describe themselves as extremely ideological. Still, the ideological tilt to the caucus attendees could advantage candidates with more ideologically extreme positions or who reflect a particular niche within the party. For example, both Jesse Jackson and Pat Robertson did better in the caucuses than primaries.[19] Yet other survey evidence finds that while caucus participants may be more ideological, they also are politically sophisticated and willing to consider the electability of candidates as well as their own issue preferences when supporting potential presidential nominees.[20]

Texas in 2008 provided a good example of the differences between a primary and a caucus, because Texas Democrats held both types of events on the same day. The presidential primary was conducted throughout the day on March 4, and results of the primary would determine the distribution of Texas' district-level delegates, which was two-thirds of its total pledged delegates. The nighttime caucuses were the first step in selecting the statewide delegates. Delegates chosen at the caucuses would attend mid-level conventions later in March and these conventions would choose delegates to attend the June state convention, where the final group of national delegates would be selected. Turnout in Texas' Democratic primary was 2.8 million voters, with Clinton winning 51 percent and Obama 48 percent of the vote. As a result, Clinton was allocated 65 delegates to Obama's 61. Participation at the nighttime caucuses was limited to those who had voted in the earlier primary, but only about one-third as many people chose to participate in the caucuses. Obama garnered greater support at the caucuses: 56 percent to Clinton's 44 percent. Thus, Obama won 38 delegates from the caucus portion to 29 for Clinton. Obama's increased support in the caucuses came from greater participation by African Americans and well-educated whites.[21] Clinton won the Texas presidential primary while Obama won in the caucuses. Adding together both components, Obama won more Texas delegates than did Clinton: 99 to 94.

In many years, caucuses receive little attention from the public, the candidates, or the media. Candidates find caucuses hard to organize, not knowing who will participate and not wanting to waste resources to recruit only a few attendees. Caucuses are often held in smaller states with fewer delegates at stake. If the candidates ignore the caucuses, the media will too. In 2008, two candidates, Obama and Romney, included the caucuses as part of their strategies. If Obama was going to overtake Clinton's frontrunner status, he would need to win every possible delegate. In the Republican caucuses, other than Iowa, Romney often was the only candidate to campaign. The tactic worked for Obama because he won in Iowa and he coupled his other caucus victories with many primary victories. The strategy failed for Romney because he lost in Iowa, the most important and competitive caucus, and he won only three primary states to go along with his seven caucus victories. Further the three primary victories were in "home" states for Romney: Michigan (where his father had been governor), Massachusetts (where Mitt Romney had been governor), and Utah (with a large contingent of Mormon voters). As such, these primary victories were discounted by the media.

Concerns over Convention Delegate Selection

Legally, the two parties' presidential nominations are bestowed at the national convention based on the count of delegates in support of each candidate. Mostly the counting of the delegate vote at the convention is pro-forma. Yet, the on-going delegate count during the conduct of the presidential primaries and caucuses determines who is the frontrunner and persuades weaker candidates to withdraw. Eventually this tally names a presumptive nominee when either 1) all other major competitors with-draw or 2) one candidate secures the backing of 50 percent of delegates. A variety of rules come into play concerning delegates. First, the two par-ties have their separate rules for dividing convention delegate totals across the 50 states (and a few territories). Second, another set of rules deter-mines how the convention delegates assigned to each state are allocated to the candidates who competed in the state's primary or caucus. Finally, a few convention delegates are selected, mostly within the Democratic Party, with no connection to the popular vote in the states. These are party and elected officials who are free to back any candidate they wish.

Apportionment of Delegates across States and Districts

In the 19th century, the Democratic and Republican parties gave each state a proportion of the convention delegates based on the size of its Electoral College vote. Thus, state delegation sizes represented popula-tion sizes to the extent that the Electoral College represented population sizes. Yet this allocation process did not match the partisan strength of each party across the states. In the late 19th and early 20th centuries the Republican Party would rarely win presidential votes from the southern states. The South was solidly Democratic. This led some to question whether the South should be equally represented at the Republican con-vention. In 1912, Taft won a contentious nomination over Roosevelt in part due to his support among the southern delegations. In 1916, the Republican Party reduced the number of convention seats given to the southern states. In 1924, it began a bonus system, where states that voted for the Republican candidate in the prior presidential election were given extra delegates. Democrats first used such a bonus system in 1944.[22]

Today, both parties allocate delegates to the states based on their popu-lation sizes and past partisan voting patterns. Republican Party rules for 2008 began by allocating each state 10 delegates, termed statewide dele-gates or delegates at large. To represent state population sizes, states were given three delegates for each seat in the House of Representatives. These are called district delegates. To reflect past partisan voting patterns an additional delegate was given to states that awarded their Electoral College vote to the Republican Party in the last presidential election. Additional delegate slots were assigned for electing Republican governors, senators, and members of the U.S. House and for holding majority party status in the state legislature. Each state also received three slots for its state party chair and its two members of the Republican National Committee. Under the Republican Party formula, Arizona received 53 delegate slots while Wisconsin, which has an equal population size, was allocated 40 delegates because it voted for fewer Republican candidates. U.S. territories, such as Guam and Puerto Rico, were allocated 59 delegates. Thus, while residents of these territories have no vote in the fall general election, they do have a role in naming the party's candidate. In all, the 2008 Republican National Convention would seat 2,381 delegates.[23]

Democratic Party rules for 2008 made initial allocations of 3,000 delegates to the states based on a formula giving equal weight to: 1) a state's Electoral College number and 2) a state's popular vote for the Democratic candidate in the last three presidential elections. Three-quarters of these state delegates would be allocated to candidates based on primary and caucus results at the congressional district level and the other one-quarter would be distributed to candidates based on statewide outcomes. In addition, U.S. territories and Americans living abroad were allotted 72 pledged delegate slots. Democratic rules also gave a state additional delegates (equivalent to 15 percent of its original total) to be filled by party officials and elected officials (PEOs) who would be bound by the state-level results of the primary. These were known as pledged PEOs. Finally, the Democratic Party provides delegate seats to party officials and high elected officials (i.e., members of Congress) who are not bound by the primary or caucus results in their states. These are the superdelegates that will be discussed later in this chapter. Thus, under Democratic rules, 3,565 bound delegates would be distributed across the states (and territories) and awarded to the presidential candidates based on their votes received in the primaries and caucuses.[24] Arizona qualified for 56 pledged delegates while Wisconsin received 74 delegates, reflecting the more Democratic orientation of Wisconsin vis-à-vis Arizona.

Are these Republican and Democratic delegate allocation formulas fair? Both parties are attempting to award delegates to states based on their population sizes and their partisan voting patterns, but each does so in a slightly different manner. One measure of "fair" would be that each convention delegate would represent the same number of potential voters in every state. Because the primaries and caucuses are used to nominate each party's presidential nomination, "fair" would more specifically mean that each delegate represented the same number of potential partisan voters.[25] Given the number of convention delegates and the potential partisan electorates in each state, a "fair" or equal distribution across all the states would have each Republican convention delegate representing the preferences of 38,719 potential voters. Because the Democratic convention has more delegates, a fair or equal distribution across the states would have each Democratic delegate represent 30,903 potential participants. An unequal distribution of convention delegates would advantage those states where each convention delegate represented fewer potential partisan participants. In other words, each of these participants received the same representation as a larger group of participants in another state.

In 2008, the number of Democratic delegates per potential Democratic voter in a state varied from 1 delegate per 11,974 Democratic residents in

Wyoming to 1 delegate per 41,866 Democratic residents in Texas. Wyoming Democrats are overrepresented because they have comparatively more delegates for a smaller number of potential voters. Texas Democrats are under represented because each of their delegates represents 3½ times as many potential Democratic voters as in Wyoming. Figure 3.1 shows the states that are most advantaged (e.g., Wyoming, Alaska, North Dakota, and Vermont) to those that are most disadvantaged (e.g., Texas, Georgia, California, and Kentucky). The most perfectly represented state is Colorado.

On the Republican side, Washington, DC residents are the most advantaged. One Republican delegate represents 2,691 potential Republican participants. As illustrated in Figure 3.2, the most disadvantaged state is California where each Republican delegate represents 74,725 potential Republican primary voters. The most perfectly represented state for its number of Republican delegates is South Carolina. The amount of variation between the advantaged (smaller number of potential voters per delegate) and the disadvantaged (larger number of potential voters per delegate) states is larger for the Republican Party than the Democratic Party.

What are the characteristics of the advantaged states? The major characteristic is population size. Smaller states do better by receiving more delegates per potential partisan voter. One way to demonstrate this is with a correlation coefficient called Pearson's r. The value of Pearson's r ranges

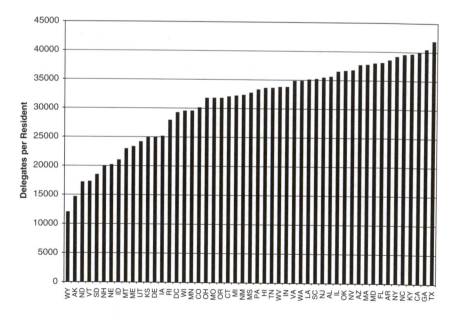

Figure 3.1 Number of delegates per Democratic resident, 2008.
Source: Calculated by author.

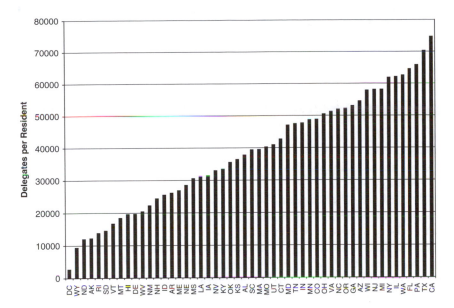

Figure 3.2 Number of Delegates per Republican resident, 2008.
Source: Calculated by author.

from 0 to 1.0. A value of 1.0 means a perfect match between two factors. A value of 0 means there is no pattern. Pearson's r also can be signed negatively or positively, depending on the direction of each factor. A second component of this measure is the level of statistical significance, which indicates whether the value of Pearson's r indicates a strength that is unlikely to occur by random chance. A good value for statistical significance is .05 (or less), because this means there is less than a 5 percent chance that the pattern is due to random chance. On the Democratic side, states with smaller populations have delegates that represent on average a smaller number of potential voters, while for larger states each delegate represents a larger number of potential primary voters (Pearson's r = .57, significance = .00). Small states do even better on the Republican side (Pearson's r = .79, significance = .00). Thus, in both parties smaller states are advantaged because each delegate represents a smaller number of voters. Larger states are disadvantaged because each delegate represents a larger number of voters.

Why do both the Democratic and Republican delegate allocation formulas produce a small-state bonus? On the Democratic side the small-state bonus arises because they measure state population sizes by votes in the Electoral College. The Electoral College has a small-state bias, because each state, regardless of size, receives two Electoral College votes to reflect representation in the U.S. Senate. The Electoral College also awards an additional vote for each member of the U.S. House of Representatives. California has the most Electoral College votes at 55, but both California voters and Wyoming voters each received an identical number of Electoral College votes for their two senators. In the Electoral College, Wyoming residents are most advantaged: each one of their state's Electoral College votes represents 165,102 residents. California is the most disadvantaged with one Electoral College vote for every 616,924 residents.[26] The Republican convention allocation formula produces a small-state bias because each state, regardless of population size, receives 10 delegate slots before adding additional delegate slots for each House seat (a measure of population size).

Were there other traits of the advantaged or disadvantaged states? Any factor related to state size would matter. In recent years, smaller states are more likely to be Republican states. For the allocation of Democratic delegates, states with a higher proportion of Republican voters actually do better than states with more Democratic voters (Pearson's r = .42, significance = .00). Thus, the Democratic formula gives more weight to states that are less likely to vote for their party's nominee in the fall election. The Republican allocation formula does not appear to have a partisan tinge to it as Pearson's r is statistically insignificant (Pearson's r = .08, significance = .56). A second factor related to state size is whether the state holds a primary or a caucus. Smaller states are more likely to opt for the caucus format. Thus, caucus states are advantaged in the delegate allocation schemes of both the Democrats (Pearson's r = −.47, significance = .00) and Republicans (Pearson's r = −.37, significance = .01).[27]

Perhaps the most important question is did these Democratic and Republican delegate allocation formulas matter for delegate support for specific candidates? Indeed, Obama did do better in the states where each delegate represented fewer potential voters. In these states which are over represented based on their potential partisan electorate, Obama earned a higher percentage of the vote (Pearson's r = −.33, significance = .02). In contrast, Clinton's supporters were disadvantaged in that she drew more of her support from the larger states which suffer from the small-state bonus in the delegate allocation formula (Pearson's r = .39, significance = .00). Obama's advantage came from winning in the smaller states which also were more likely to be the caucus states. On the Republican side in contests through Super Tuesday, John McCain faired poorly from the delegate allocation scheme (Pearson's r = .48, significance = .01) because he polled better in larger states and he did not actively contest most of the caucus states. On the other hand, support for neither Romney (Pearson's r = −.07, significance = .75) nor Huckabee (Pearson's r = −.21, significance = .30) seemed to be affected by any biases in the Republican allocation of delegates across the states. Such candidate advantages, however, are not confined to the presidential nomination process. The small-state bonus in the Electoral College contributed to the results of the 2000 presidential election. Without the small-state bonus, George W. Bush would have lost in the Electoral College by 14 votes![28] Thus, U.S. presidential elections have the same small-state bias in the general election (i.e., the Electoral College) as in the nomination phase (i.e., the allocation of delegates across the states).

Punishments and Bonuses in Delegate Allocations

In 2008, both parties punished states which violated the party rules on selection of dates for their primaries or caucuses. Republican Party rules did not allow any state to choose delegates prior to February. Under these rules the primaries in New Hampshire, Michigan, South Carolina, and Florida were held too early, and each of these states lost half of their delegate totals. Wyoming also lost half of its delegates for selecting delegates through a caucus held in January. Since the caucuses held in Iowa and Nevada did not select any national convention delegates (these would be selected at later state conventions), those two states were not punished. Despite being stripped of half their delegates, the four primaries did not lose their importance in the 2008 Republican contests. Victories in New Hampshire and South Carolina gave McCain the early boost he needed to make him the frontrunner going into Super Tuesday. Meanwhile, Fred Thompson's loss in South Carolina and Rudy Giuliani's loss in Florida ended their candidacies. Taking away half of the delegates was not a sufficient punishment to preclude these states from adopting early primary dates. Further, because of these early dates, these four states played crucial roles in providing momentum to McCain's candidacy while eliminating other candidates from the field.

The Democratic Party attempted to impose more severe punishment than the Republicans. Under Democratic rules the Michigan and Florida primaries were scheduled too early. In an initial ruling, the Democratic Party stripped these two states of all of their delegates and the presidential candidates were instructed not to campaign in these states. Most of the candidates removed their name from the Michigan ballot, though Hillary Clinton's name remained. In the Michigan primary Clinton won 55 percent of the vote and 40 percent was designated as "uncommitted." In Florida, the candidates' names remained on the ballot, with Clinton receiving 50 percent and Obama 33 percent of the vote. But no delegates were awarded from either state. As the national contest between Clinton and Obama remained close, Clinton backers increasingly lobbied for some of the Florida and Michigan delegates to be restored. Party officials also feared that Florida and Michigan voters might refuse to vote for the Democratic nominee in the fall election in retaliation for being denied a voice in the nomination process. On May 31, 2008, the Democratic National Committee partially reversed itself and awarded half a vote to each delegate from Michigan and Florida. Clinton was allocated 35 delegates from Michigan and 52 from Florida, while Obama received 29 Michigan and 39 Florida delegates. After this adjustment, the size of the 2008 Democratic convention changed to 3,410 pledged delegates.

In 2008, the Democratic Party attempted to encourage states to hold later primaries. States would be given bonus delegates if they held their primary or caucus after March 31.[29] Eight states, Puerto Rico, and Guam qualified for these bonus delegates receiving on average an additional five delegates. The largest number of bonus delegates was 24 awarded to North Carolina which held its primary on May 6. The Democratic Party's bonus plan had little influence on stemming the tide toward early primaries. Likewise, a bonus delegate scheme adopted by the Republican Party for its 2000 convention also failed to convince states to hold later primaries.

Bonus delegates are not sufficient incentives for states to hold late primaries, because in most recent presidential nomination contests the national race between the candidates is over before these late primaries are held. Likewise, punishing states for going early by taking away half of their delegates is not a sufficient disincentive. Candidates use the earliest contests to capture a leading spot in the national contests between the candidates not to accumulate delegates. An early victory, or two, secures entry into the second round of primaries. It is in this second round, which in recent years is often the first of several "super" Tuesdays, that candidates' attention turns to delegate totals. Trying to control the primary and caucus calendar has proven to be a difficult task for both the Democratic and Republican parties.

Superdelegates

Among the more controversial elements of the 2008 Democratic allocation formula was the unpledged PEOs, which are more commonly referred to as superdelegates. These superdelegates included members of the Democratic National Committee (DNC), and Democratic senators, U.S. representatives, and governors. Past Democratic presidents, vice presidents, leaders of the House and Senate, and prior DNC chairs also are included. Superdelegates are not required to vote for presidential candidates based on the results of the primaries or caucuses in their states. Superdelegates could announce their support for a presidential contender at any time, change their support during the campaign, or withhold their support until after the primaries were over. After restoring half of the superdelegate totals to Florida and Michigan, the Democratic Party would have 826 superdelegates in 2008, just shy of 20 percent of the final count of 4,235 convention delegates.

Superdelegates were created by the Democratic Party to be a part of its 1984 convention. This countermanded an earlier McGovern-Fraser Commission guideline that prohibited ex officio delegates, that is delegates who obtained their slots simply because of the offices they held. A Democratic governor under the McGovern-Fraser rules could still be a convention delegate, but he or she would have to be selected as a delegate supporting a presidential candidate in the same manner as other party activists. What happened between 1972 and 1984 to change the minds of the leaders of the Democratic Party? First, the number of Democratic delegates who were governors, senators, or members of the House of Representatives declined sharply with the earlier ban on ex officio delegates. In 1968, 92 percent of all Democratic governors were delegates to the convention, as well as 67 percent of Democratic senators and 36 percent of House members. At the 1976 Democratic convention, only 44 percent of the Democratic governors, 18 percent of the senators, and 15 percent of House members were delegates.[30] Some party leaders simply felt that the participation of the party's elected officials was important for the wisdom they might have from their years in office. Further, having the party's senators and House members play a role in the presidential nomination would begin an alliance between the party's members in Congress and the hopefully future president.

The second factor that led to the switch in Democratic Party rules, and the creation of superdelegate slots, was the outcome of the 1980 election. President Jimmy Carter lost badly to Ronald Reagan in his reelection bid, and Democrats lost seats in the House and lost control of the Senate to the Republicans. Four years earlier, Jimmy Carter had gone from being a little-known former governor of Georgia to the Democratic Party's presidential nominee by winning a series of primaries. Carter never had much support from the party's establishment. When Carter failed to be an effective president and lost his reelection bid, renewed calls came forth for a greater voice for the party's elite in influencing the presidential nominations.[31]

The new superdelegates proved to be controversial for the 1984 Democratic nomination. Former vice president Walter Mondale secured the support of many of these superdelegates before any primary votes were cast. Mondale's major opponents, Gary Hart and Jesse Jackson, felt short-changed. At the national convention, Mondale won the nomination with the support of 56 percent of all the delegates. Included in this total were 79 percent of the superdelegates. Without this support, Mondale's delegate count would have shrunk to 52 percent.[32] The Democratic Party established yet another reform commission after 1984 to look into the matter of superdelegates, but failed to make any major changes. Many in the party had simply grown tired of continually changing the rules.[33] The role of the superdelegates was less controversial in the 1988–2004 Democratic nominations, because these nominations were won by one candidate winning decisive victories in a series of primaries. A close race in 2008 would bring superdelegates back to the center of the debate over nomination rules.

With headlines such as "Superdelegates Could Prove Kingmakers," or "In Background, a Battle for Superdelegates," media stories debated whether superdelegates would decide the 2008 nomination.[34] A close race in pledged delegates selected from the primaries and caucuses could place superdelegates in a position to decide the nomination. Thus, both Obama and Clinton actively courted the support of these delegates. Besides adding to the candidates' overall delegate totals, the endorsement from a super-delegate who was a prominent senator or governor could be particularly newsworthy. Such was the case when Senator Ted Kennedy endorsed Obama. Some superdelegates endorsed early, some waited.

During the invisible primary stage and the first two months of 2008, Hillary Clinton led Obama in superdelegates. This reflected Clinton's longer presence on the national stage. She had more connections with the party's elite which make up the superdelegates. In addition, many party elite were initially reluctant to back Obama, who had only served in the Senate for two years before he declared his candidacy. Once Obama began to win in the primaries and caucuses, he gained strength among the super-delegates. Figure 3.3 charts the delegate totals of Obama and Clinton, with one set of lines representing the pledged delegates won from primary

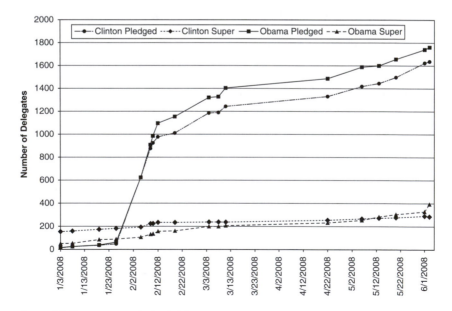

Figure 3.3 Democratic pledged delegates and superdelegates, 2008.
Source: Delegate totals from CNN webpages.

and caucus victories and a second set representing support from superdelegates. In January, Clinton led Obama in superdelegate endorsements by 154 to 50. Through mid-February, Obama picked up 111 superdelegates while Clinton added only 80. The trend continued in March as Obama's superdelegate support grew by 45 while Clinton added only four to her total. Even though Clinton was winning important primaries in Ohio and Texas in March and Pennsylvania in April, Obama continued to pick up more superdelegate support than Clinton. Obama surpassed Clinton in total superdelegate support in the second week of May. On the morning of the last two primaries on June 3, a handful of superdelegates came forward with endorsements of Obama. These superdelegates plus the pledged delegates Obama won by winning in Montana and finishing second to Clinton in South Dakota pushed Obama past the required 50 percent of Democratic convention delegates needed to clinch the nomination. While much of the speculation in 2008 was whether the superdelegates would help Clinton win the nomination, even if Obama might have more pledged delegates, in the end the superdelegates helped Obama to win the last few delegate votes needed to secure the nomination.

The Republican Party does not have delegates that are called superdelegates. They do set aside three delegate slots from each state for the state party chair and the state's two members of the Republican National Committee. In 2008, these ex officio delegates comprised 6 percent of the convention total. In a small number of states, state party rules require these ex officio members to vote according to the primary results.[35] The Republican Party, in general, has a variety of uncommitted delegates at its national conventions, whether they are chosen by caucuses or at state conventions or are ex officio delegates.

The Democratic Party's superdelegates put a public face on the party elite with formal attendance at the national convention. The Republican Party also has a significant number of its party's elected officials selected as convention delegates. Even without this formal role, the two parties' elites shape the course of the nomination race. As Cohen et al. describe in their book *The Party Decides*, the two parties' elected officials, major donors, and activists lend crucial support to candidates during the invisible primary stage. If the party elite coalesce around one candidate, this candidate becomes a strong frontrunner before any votes are cast.[36]

Winning Votes Versus Winning Pledged Delegates

In all of the Democratic presidential primaries and most of those on the Republican side, voters mark a ballot to indicate which of the national candidates they support. One voter marks the ballot for Obama, another for Clinton. Yet, like in the fall presidential election, voters are actually voting for a group of people to represent their preferences at a later date.

In the fall presidential election, a vote for Obama is a vote for the state's Democratic slate of electors. If Obama wins the state's popular vote, his slate of electors will meet at the state capital in December to officially cast the state's ballots in the Electoral College. In the presidential primaries, a vote for one of the candidates is actually a vote for potential delegates who will support that candidate at the national convention.

The question becomes how to distribute convention delegate slots to the candidates based on the primary vote. In the Electoral College model, all but two American states use a winner-take-all provision: the candidate with the most votes receives all the Electoral College votes. Two states, Maine and Nebraska, distribute two of the Electoral College votes to the statewide winner and the remaining electors go to the winning candidate in each congressional district. In the general election, the winner-take-all model works reasonably well because in most years only two candidates, the Democratic and Republican candidates, have any realistic chance of winning the presidential election. With only two candidates, one candidate is more likely to win an absolute majority of the vote. Yet, a candidate only needs to be the plurality winner (getting more votes than any other candidate) to win the state's Electoral College votes. So in some cases, a candidate will win all of a state's Electoral College votes with less than a majority vote.

In presidential primaries, the contest is often between more than two candidates, especially in the early primary states. One candidate might win 35 percent of the vote, another 30 percent, and the remaining one-third of the vote may be distributed between two or more other candidates. In such a scenario, the awarding of all of a state's delegates to the candidate with the most votes may not seem as fair. On the other hand, awarding delegates by winner-take-all rules could lead the party to more quickly consolidate support behind one leading candidate.

The Democratic Party struggled in the 1980s over what was the best method to use to distribute delegates to candidates based on their vote totals. The party banned winner-take-all primaries for its 1976 convention. Instead, party reformers felt that proportional representation rules would be the fairest. If a candidate won the support of 40 percent of the voters in the primary, the candidate would be awarded 40 percent of the state's Democratic convention delegates. Proportional representation rules have been the dominant method for distribution of Democratic Party delegates since 1976, but the party allowed a few alternative methods in the 1980s before settling on a consistent use of proportional representation rules for all Democratic primaries and caucuses in 1992. Democratic rules further require a candidate to win a minimum of 15 percent of the vote in order to receive any delegates. Finally, Democratic rules distribute one-quarter of a state's delegates to candidates based on the statewide vote and the other three-quarters of the delegates based on voting results in the separate congressional districts.[37]

Table 3.2 Delegate distribution rules for the 2008 Republican primaries and caucuses

Distribution rule	Primaries	Caucuses
Winner-take-all statewide	12	2
Winner-take-all if majority vote	4	2
Winner-take-all separately at state level and congressional district level	10	0
Proportional representation	9	1
Direct election of delegates	2	0
No formal rules	0	9

Source: Rhodes Cook, *Race for the Presidency: Winning the 2008 Nomination* (Washington, DC: CQ Press, 2008).

The Republican Party has not imposed a national standard for the allocating of delegates to candidates. Commentators often focus on the winner-take-all rules on the Republican side, but the picture is much more complicated. Table 3.2 shows the variety of delegate formats used by the Republican Party in 2008. Twelve of the Republican primaries did allocate delegates by the winner-take-all method to the candidate winning the statewide vote. Thus, John McCain won all 58 of Missouri's delegates even though the statewide popular vote results were 33.0 percent for McCain, 31.5 percent for Huckabee, and 29.3 percent for Romney. In four states, a candidate could win all of the state's delegates but only if that candidate won an absolute majority (i.e., 50 percent) of the popular vote or in the case of Tennessee, two-thirds of the vote. In none of these states did one candidate win the required number of the votes, so the winner-take-all rules did not apply. In three of the states, delegates were distributed under proportional representation rules and in Louisiana delegates were chosen at the state convention, instead.

Ten states also used winner-take-all rules, but they separated the vote between delegates selected on the basis of the statewide vote and delegates selected at the congressional district level. Remember, the Republican formula allocates three delegates per congressional district. In this split-level winner-take-all format, several candidates can receive delegates if different candidates win the vote from different areas of the state. Thus in Georgia, Mike Huckabee won the statewide vote at 33.9 percent to 31.6 percent for McCain and 30.2 for Romney. If Georgia had a simple statewide winner-take-all, he would have won 72 delegates. With delegates distributed by both the statewide and congressional district results, Huckabee won 54 delegates, McCain was the plurality winner in four congressional districts and earned 12 delegates, and Romney won in two congressional districts receiving 6 delegates. However, if one candidate won both the statewide vote and the vote in all of the congressional districts, that candidate would win all of the state's convention delegates. Such was the case in Maryland. McCain won 54.8 percent of the statewide vote and was the plurality victor in each of the eight congressional districts. McCain was allocated all 37 of Maryland's Republican delegates.

Nine states used proportional representation rules for the Republican Party primary as well as for the Democratic primary. In addition, in two states proportional representation rules were used for the allocation of the statewide delegates, but the congressional district delegates were distributed on winner-take-all rules. In two more states Republican voters cast their ballots directly for people running to be convention delegates. In Illinois, those running to be convention delegates indicate which presidential candidate they would support, but in Pennsylvania, there was no such designation. Direct election of convention delegates is the oldest format for a presidential primary and was quite common during the earlier part of the 20th century. Republican Party caucuses could be held under any of these rules, but mostly, there were no formal rules at all. The participants at each local caucus decided how to select the delegates.

2008 Delegate Totals under Alternative Distribution Schemes

Did the more complicated rules of the Republican primary really matter in the long run in 2008? Did the Democratic Party proportional representation rules stretch out the contest? Did these rules disadvantage Hillary Clinton who won in many of the large-state primaries but received only a few more delegates than Obama when they were distributed proportionately? Former president Bill Clinton sure thought so, arguing Senator Clinton would have been ahead of Obama in delegates after the Pennsylvania primary if the party used winner-take-all rules. Other commentators chimed in arguing that proportional representation rules were prolonging the Democratic contest and disadvantaging Senator Clinton, while the Republican rules were lauded as efficiently bringing that race to a close.[38]

Mathematically, the number of delegates won in each state can be redistributed across the candidates by using the presidential preference vote for each of the candidates. Both journalists and academics have recalculated convention delegates using this method. The procedure that would show the most extreme results is to reallocate convention delegates based on the statewide vote either entirely by winner-take-all or entirely by a simple proportional distribution (without a minimum requirement). This is not a realistic scenario because neither party used purely proportional representation or purely winner-take-all rules based solely on statewide results. However, it is the method of calculation that will show the most dramatic results.

Table 3.3 Republican delegate accumulation under different rules

	Winner-take-all			Proportional representation		
	McCain	Romney	Huckabee	McCain	Romney	Huckabee
Feb. 2	93	82	37	55	73	38
Feb. 5	664	313	252	422	425	238
March 4	1108		314	682		416

Source: Calculated by author.

Table 3.3 shows the cumulative Republican delegate totals for McCain, Romney, and Huckabee at three time periods.[39] The first is February 2, which would include results from the first seven primaries or caucuses. Few delegates are selected during these early events, in part because many of these states were penalized for holding their primary or caucus outside the prescribed rules for the Republican Party. Under the winner-take-all scenario, McCain holds an 11 delegate lead over Romney with Huckabee trailing by more than 50 delegates. If all of these events had used proportional representation rules, Romney would have led McCain by 18 delegates. After Super Tuesday, a greater disparity in results appears. Under winner-take-all rules McCain leads Romney by 351 delegates; under proportional representation Romney leads McCain by 3 delegates. The Republican delegate race would have been much closer after Super Tuesday if proportional representation rules had been used.

In reality after Super Tuesday, the actual delegate count, as reported on CNN webpages, showed McCain ahead of Romney 680 to 270. At this point, Romney dropped out of the race. Huckabee remained in the contest until McCain amassed 50 percent of the Republican delegates on March 4. Under any of the scenarios, Huckabee would not have overtaken McCain, but under proportional representation McCain would not have achieved the 50 percent delegate total at the beginning of March.

How could McCain do so much better under winner-take-all than proportional representation rules? The Super Tuesday results are the best illustration. McCain won 9 of the 15 Republican primaries on February 5. This included large states such as California, New Jersey, and New York. The states McCain won on Super Tuesday allocated 593 delegates. Romney won only two primaries on Super Tuesday: Massachusetts and Utah which allocated 79 delegates. Romney did win the caucus states on Super Tuesday but these allocate fewer delegates and often the actual delegates are selected much later at a state convention. McCain loses delegates under a proportional representation system because he averaged 45 percent of the vote in the nine states that he won. That means that the other 55 percent of the delegates would be awarded to another candidate.

Romney picks up a good portion of these delegates, plus he maintains a lead in caucus state delegates. McCain did not contest these caucuses and won only a small portion of the votes.

The Republican rules, which on Super Tuesday came closer to the winner-take-all model than the proportional representation model, favored McCain. Romney dropped out because he trailed significantly in the delegate totals. Yet, Romney's campaign displayed other weaknesses. Romney won only three primaries: Michigan, Massachusetts, and Utah. All three of these could be considered his home field: he was the former governor of Massachusetts, his father had been governor in Michigan, and many Utah voters shared Romney's Mormon faith. A candidate needs to win outside of his home states and own region of the country to remain a viable candidate for the nomination. Romney failed to do so. Meanwhile, McCain was winning in the Northeast (New Hampshire, New York, and New Jersey), the South (South Carolina), the Midwest (Illinois, Missouri) and the West (California).

Different delegate distributions also would alter totals for the two Democratic candidates in 2008. Under a strict state-level winner-take-all scenario, Hillary Clinton wins the nomination as illustrated in Figure 3.4. After Super Tuesday, Clinton is ahead of Obama 1,072 delegates to 753. Obama takes the lead on February 12, after his string of caucus and primary victories. Clinton retakes the lead on March 4 with victories in

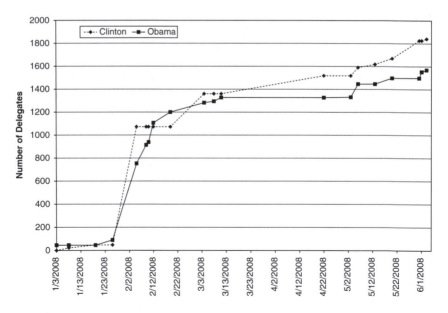

Figure 3.4 Democratic delegate accumulation under winner-take-all rules, 2008.
Source: Calculated by author.

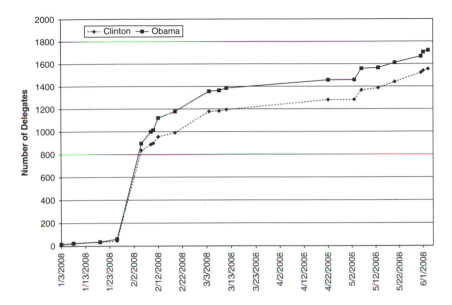

Figure 3.5 Democratic delegate accumulation under proportional representation rules, 2008.

Source: Calculated by author.

Ohio, Rhode Island, and the primary portion of Texas. At the end of the all the primaries and caucuses, Clinton leads Obama by 272 delegates. A proportional representation distribution based solely on statewide results, as illustrated in Figure 3.5, shows Obama winning the nomination. These hypothetical statewide proportional representation results come closer to the actual outcome because the Democratic rules are proportional representation but at both the district and statewide levels.

How much did proportional representation rules matter in the 2008 Democratic race? Once again a focus on Super Tuesday presents a good case. Clinton won the California primary with 52 percent of the statewide vote. Under Democratic Party rules, she won 203 delegates to Obama's 167. Under statewide winner-take-all, Clinton would have gained 370 delegates from California. The same scenario occurs in Massachusetts. Instead of winning all 93 delegates, Clinton who scored 56 percent of the vote in the primary was allocated 55 delegates to Obama's 38.

Such mathematical manipulations of delegate distribution rules have been shown to affect the outcome of earlier presidential nomination contests.[40] Yet these scenarios do not reflect reality. First, neither party uses strict statewide winner-take-all or proportional representation rules. Brian Arbour reran the 2008 Democratic contest using the actual

Republican Party rules in each state and found Clinton to have only a four vote lead in delegates over Obama at the end of the primaries. The remaining delegates (using Republican rules) would be selected at a small number of state conventions held during the summer. The Democratic race under Republican rules would have extended into the summer.[41] Second, even an exact match to the real rules cannot fully judge how the outcome would be altered by different rules. The existing rules affect candidates' strategies. With winner-take-all rules, candidates will ignore contests that are expected to be lopsided, either for or against them. Candidates' time and money are better spent in states where the competing candidates' projected support is evenly matched. In such states, moving a small percentage of the electorate to push a candidate's total over 50 percent produces a gain of all the state's delegates. This is the campaign strategy that the Electoral College produces in the general election. Under proportional representation, candidates will seek out pockets of support in most of the states. Rules matter, but so do candidate strategies.

The Accidental Calendar, Part I: Iowa and New Hampshire Come First

No master plan created the present calendar for the presidential primaries and caucuses. As is true for most election laws, the dates of the primaries or caucuses are left up to the states. Since the 1970s, the national parties have set a beginning date for the primaries. At first, this beginning date requirement for the Democratic Party was that delegates must be selected within the election year. Since 1980, the Democratic Party has established a "window" of allowable dates, listing a starting and ending date for primaries. In 2008, the Democratic window spanned from February 5 through June 10. Exemptions were given to Iowa and New Hampshire, which by historical accident had events scheduled at the start of the primary calendar, and for Nevada and South Carolina, to provide a wider demographic base to the earliest contests. The Republican Party set their calendar window in 2008 from February 5 through July 28, with no exceptions for earlier events. States that selected dates outside of these windows were punished by having delegates taken away from them.

Prior to the reforms of the 1970s, holding an early primary or caucus was not very important. In the period after World War II, candidates selectively chose among the 16 or so states that held presidential primaries. Some candidates did not run in any primaries, waiting to show their strengths at the national convention. Other candidates, usually those with something to prove, contested some but usually not all of the primaries. In most states, candidates seeking the nomination request to be placed on the primary ballot, usually by obtaining a required number of voters' signatures on a petition. In these states, the primary ballot in the post-World War II era might list one, two, or none of the national candidates. Sometimes a state's primary ballot listed only a favorite-son candidate. A handful of primary states guaranteed competitive races by having a state official list all the candidates on the ballot. The competitive primaries, in which two or more national candidates competed, became the important primaries regardless of where they occurred on the primary calendar. In 1960 the Wisconsin primary on April 5 was the key battle ground between John Kennedy and Hubert Humphrey, while in 1964 Barry Goldwater's victory over Nelson Rockefeller in California's June 2 primary helped Goldwater secure the nomination. If the election calendar mattered at all, the last round of primaries often became the most important. A win in California's June primary could lift a candidate's fortunes going into the summer conventions. After all, during this period the point of a primary victory was to convince the party's elite at the convention that a candidate could win the support of voters.

New Hampshire enacted its presidential law in 1913, the same time other states were adopting this new reform. Before its first presidential primary in 1916, New Hampshire moved the date of the primary to the second Tuesday in March to coincide with their Town Meetings. In 1916, several other states held primaries on the same day or earlier, but in subsequent years these states either moved their primary dates back or discontinued primaries all together. New Hampshire had the early date to itself. The New Hampshire primary for the first 36 years was a direct election of delegates primary. Voters chose among numerous local residents bidding for slots as delegates. Delegates elected were officially uncommitted with respect to the national candidates, though many would make their candidate preference known.

In 1952, New Hampshire adopted a nonbinding preference primary to accompany the delegate election ballot. Voters could now cast a ballot for a preferred national candidate, but the selection of delegates was not connected to this vote nor were the delegates selected bound to following the results from the preference ballot. Still, this new preference ballot added enough pizzazz to the New Hampshire primary to draw in the attention of the national candidates and media. A victory in the 1952 Republican primary helped start Dwight Eisenhower's bid for the nomination, even though he did not personally campaign in the state. In 1977, New Hampshire dropped the direct election of delegates portion of the primary ballot, leaving only the presidential preference vote which would now be linked to the selection of delegates.[42]

After the nomination reforms of the 1970s, and the subsequent proliferation of the primaries, holding an early primary became more important. Now candidates would run in all the primaries and an early victory would add to a candidate's reputation and bring in additional resources, such as campaign contributions. Equally as important, candidates who did not do well began to drop out of the race. By the 1980s, nomination races often were over by the middle of the primary election calendar. While voters in states with late primaries often did not have any choices at all, New Hampshire voters always got a chance to choose among all the national candidates. Further, candidates spent considerable amounts of time in New Hampshire, hoping to obtain a victory. This intensive campaigning benefited the state economically. Candidates' campaigns spent money on advertisements, food and hotels, telephone connections, and temporary local campaign offices. Media coverage of the candidates campaigning provided free publicity for the state. Being first was good. To retain this advantage, New Hampshire began to pass a series of laws in the 1970s to place its primary before any other.

Iowa's journey to the front of the line also was a historical accident. The local caucus meetings are the first of a series of events. For example, in 2008, those who attended the 2,166 local caucuses (held on January 3) chose from among themselves delegates to go to 99 county conventions (held on March 15). The county conventions selected delegates to go to six congressional district conventions (held on April 26). At these district conventions, a portion of the delegates to the national convention are chosen and additional delegates are selected to attend a state convention. The state convention (held on June 28) names the remaining delegates for the national convention. In 1972, the Democratic national convention had an early date of July 9. Iowa state party rules required 30 days between events, such as between the local caucuses and the county conventions. To fit all of the intervening events between the caucuses and the national convention within the 30-day spacing requirement, the 1972 Iowa caucuses needed to be held no later than January 24. This put the Iowa caucuses ahead of the New Hampshire primary. In 1976 the Iowa Republican Party joined the early caucus date.

The second part of the Iowa story is a combination of candidate strategies and media coverage. In 1972, the Iowa caucus received a small amount of attention from the candidates and the national media. Iowa became more of a story in 1976 when Jimmy Carter used an Iowa "victory" to launch his successful bid for the Democratic nomination. Carter did not actually win in Iowa; he placed second to "uncommitted." Carter was able to use his limited resources to capture a win in Iowa and gain publicity. Since the 1970s, Iowa has become a requisite stop for Democratic hopefuls. Iowa has not been as essential on the Republican side, and several successful candidates (Ronald Reagan, John McCain) avoided (or claimed to be avoiding) the Iowa caucuses. As a result, the media did not fault them for doing poorly in the caucuses.[43]

Criticisms of early dates for Iowa and New Hampshire are numerous and frequently made. These are two small states. New Hampshire's population is the same size as Phoenix's. Iowa and New Hampshire are not representative of the nation as a whole. Neither state has many minority residents or any large cities. Yet, candidates spend considerable time campaigning in these small states. In 2000, McCain's victory in New Hampshire was predicated on 60 days of campaign events. Further, candidates cater to the parochial issues of these two states. In Iowa, both Democratic and Republican candidates endorse ethanol, made from corn, as an alternative fuel source.[44] Finally, critics argue it is unfair for the same two states to always lead off the nomination calendar, giving them undue influence over the nomination outcomes.

Supporters of Iowa and New Hampshire argue the two states are small enough for "retail" politics. With numerous candidate visits, individual citizens and local party activists are able to personally meet the candidates. Equally as important, the candidates talk to real people and learn about their concerns. In larger states, candidate strategies are confined to media advertisements and a few short visits or large-scale rallies. Supporters of Iowa and New Hampshire also argue that the two states are not as unrepresentative as often portrayed and that any two states will not be perfect microcosms of the nation as a whole.[45]

The Accidental Calendar, Part 2: The Perils of Front-Loading

With the change in candidate strategies after the 1970s reform, holding an early primary or caucus became more important. Voters in early contests could choose among all the national candidates. Candidates who faired poorly dropped out, leaving fewer choices for subsequent primary voters. Eventually, all the competitors except the eventual victor would drop out. By the 1980s, the competitive phase of the nomination contest often ended by mid-March. States holding late primaries had no voice in these nominations.

States had numerous reasons for moving their primary dates forward. Most were seeking more clout for their state. Candidates must court voters in early primary states. In doing so, candidates may tailor at least part of their issue positions to match those of voters in the early primary states. Efforts by states to create regional primaries, and place them early on the election calendar, also contributed to front-loading. Some states also moved the date of their primary forward in hopes of assisting a particular candidate, as Georgia did in 1976 to bolster Carter's candidacy. Other state leaders resented candidates coming to their states to raise funds, only to spend them in Iowa or New Hampshire. California governor Arnold Schwarzenegger expressed such frustration: "Candidates only came here to California to cash in. They went from fundraiser to fundraiser. Made millions and millions of dollars, and before the fundraiser was over, they were already on the plane leaving for New Hampshire and Iowa to spend the millions of dollars they had cashed in California ... this drives me nuts."[46] Once some states began to move their primary date forward, it became harder for other states to resist.

With front-loading, more Tuesdays become Super Tuesdays as states congregate on the few available early dates. The whole nomination process speeds up. Voters have less time to learn about the candidates. They barely have time to digest the results of Iowa before New Hampshire holds its primaries, and then another group of primaries is on the heels of New Hampshire. The process gives extra weight to early results, such as in 2004 where Kerry's victories in Iowa and New Hampshire established him as the frontrunner and led him to a quick round of victories in subsequent primaries. Voters in the early primary states may be rushed to judgment. Voters in later primary states may have no voice at all. In 1988, one-third of the primaries occurred after candidates became the presumptive nominee for their party; in 2000, three-fifths of primaries occurred after the major competitors to Bush and Gore had withdrawn. When McCain secured the position of the Republican's presumptive nominee in 2008, one-half of the primaries had not been held. With the nomination decision already secure, fewer voters participate in the late primary states.[47]

Front-loading affects the candidates as well. The congested primary schedule requires candidates to raise larger and larger sums of money earlier and earlier. Jimmy Carter raised slightly less than a million dollars prior to 1976. In 1983 Walter Mondale's frontrunner position was secured with a $9.7 million total. Before 1996, Robert Dole's war chest stood at $24.6 million. By 2000, George W. Bush raised the stakes for a frontrunner to $68 million, and before 2008, both Clinton and Obama each amassed $100 million. Candidates unable to keep up with these rising costs of the campaign are unable to compete effectively. Candidates who do remain in the fray are forced into a superficial form of campaigning as their resources are stretched thin by contesting multiple contests on the same day or within a short period of time. Candidates jet from one stop to another, delivering the same stump speech, with little true interaction with the voters. The congested, front-loaded primary calendar has been one of the major impetuses for renewed calls for presidential primary reform.

A Hodgepodge of Rules and Procedures

The presidential nomination process in the first three election cycles in the 21st century had many peculiar rules. The nomination process was neither consistent nor logical. As the discussion of the history of presidential nominations in Chapter 1 revealed, today's nomination process sandwiches together the traditional national conventions with a more contemporary focus on citizen participation through primaries and caucuses. Many elements are left under the control of state governments or state parties producing vast variations in the structures from state to state and year to year. The front-loaded calendar came about from individual states vying for more power. State laws or parties determine whether an open or closed primary is held or whether a primary or a caucus format is used. The national parties try to shape the overall process, with rules on allowable primary dates, formats for allocating delegates across states, and in the Democratic case, rules for distributing delegates based on vote totals. Still, with so many rule makers, and no dictators, a hodgepodge of structures results.

Nomination politics is made up of more than the state laws and party rules. Candidate strategies and missteps in those strategies affect nomination outcomes as much as the election calendar or delegate allocation rules. Giuliani postponing his entry into the 2008 Republican contest until Florida cleared the way for McCain, or another candidate, to secure an earlier frontrunner position. Media practices also shape the overall dynamics of the nomination process. The media over-cover Iowa and New Hampshire, because these are the first real votes for the candidates. Yet in doing so, the media make those two small states even more important in the nomination outcomes. The media also are quick to call winners and losers in individual primaries, fundraising totals, or public opinion poll standings. The media are quick to call winners and losers in many election contests and in the give-and-take of the policy process between the president and Congress. The media in every election give more attention to horse-race elements, such as who's ahead in fundraising or whose campaign staff might be bickering among themselves, than in reporting the issue positions of the candidates. Reporters, and publishers, believe that the public finds the horse-race components more interesting than issue positions. In addition, horse-race aspects of an electoral contest change over time while candidate issue positions do not.[48]

Changes to state laws or party rules cannot dictate to candidates their ultimate strategies, though these new laws or rules would alter the optimum strategies for many candidates. Legal changes also would not control how the media cover elections. At best, reporters would look for new indicators of who's ahead and who's behind. Still, many observers of the current presidential nomination process find it too messy and too biased. Thus, the call for additional reforms. Most of these focus on changing the election calendar. Chapter 4 will highlight the arguments for and against many of these proposed reforms.

Alternative Methods for Nominating Presidents

Presidential nominations at the start of the 21st century were won by a process that was both complicated and flawed, but would any other method be better? Numerous alternatives have been proposed. Many of the ideas are not new. For example, the proposal to switch to a single national presidential primary dates back to the early years of the 20th century. Grouping presidential primaries by region was first suggested in the 1970s. More recently, the Republican Party in 2000 seriously considered a plan to group primaries by state population sizes. Each proposal offers what its advocates see as a more rational method for selecting nominees for the country's highest elective office. Yet, each proposal has its own set of potential flaws and likely unintended consequences. How any of these reforms would be adopted is an additional complicating factor.

The impetus for these calls to once again reform the presidential nomination process was problems with the 2000–2008 election calendars. These calendars of presidential primaries and caucuses had no grand plan to organize the procession from an election in one state to the next. The preeminent role of Iowa and New Hampshire was questioned for the fairness of the same two states always leading off the nomination calendar and for the unrepresentative nature of their electorates. The increasingly front-loaded calendar brought up additional concerns. Too many primaries sandwiched on the same date increased the costs of campaigning and disadvantaged lesser known or less well-financed candidates. Further, with so many primaries scheduled at the front end of the nomination calendar, the nomination contest often was over before citizens in states with later primaries had a chance to vote. Such concerns led politicians, party activists, advocacy groups, journalists, and social scientists to call for new reforms to rationalize the calendar of presidential primaries and caucuses.

In this chapter, the major reform proposals will be examined for their potential benefits and problems. The first set will be those plans to restructure the primary calendar by grouping states by region, across regions or by population size. The alternative to these grouping methods is switching to a single national primary. While a national primary would appear to be a simple and direct method to nominate candidates, it brings along concerns over how to tally the vote when the list of candidates extends to four, five, or more individuals. The chapter will conclude with a section on the difficulties of adopting major reforms.

Regional Primary Plans

The first proposal for a regional primary was introduced into Congress by Robert Packwood (D-OR) in 1972. His plan divided the country into five regions. Every state within a region would hold its primary on the same date. The ordering of the regions would be determined by a lottery. The first group of primaries would be held on the first Tuesday in March and the last regional primary would be scheduled for the first Tuesday in July. In most years since Packwood's original proposal a regional primary plan, or two, has been introduced into Congress. Most of these plans are similar, varying between four and six regions and using a system of rotating the order of regions across election years.

In the 110th Congress, the regional bill was introduced as the Regional Presidential Primary and Caucus Act of 2007 (HR 3487, S. 1905) with four Florida Democratic representatives (Alcee Hastings, Kathy Castor, Kendrick Meek, and Debbie Wasserman Schultz) sponsoring the legislation in the House and Senators Amy Klobuchar (D-MN), Lamar Alexander (R-TN), and Joseph Lieberman (I-CT) sponsoring the Senate version. This latest congressional proposal has four regions; primaries or caucuses scheduled for the first Tuesdays in March, April, May and June; and the order of the regions to be determined by a lottery. Figure 4.1 shows a map of this regional primary proposal.

Since 1999, the National Association of Secretaries of State (NASS) also has supported the regional primary format. Their plan includes four regions and rotation of regions. Unlike the congressional plan, the NASS version allows Iowa and New Hampshire to hold their events prior to the four regions. The rationale is to allow lesser known candidates to compete in these smaller states in advance of the larger regional groupings of states. The NASS proposal has been endorsed by a number of other intergovernmental organizations representing state governments and election reform.[1] A slight variant on the rotating regional primary plans is a regional lottery plan, as proposed by political scientist Larry Sabato.[2] The ordering of the four regions in each year would be determined by a lottery held on January 1. The short notice of the ordering for the regions in each election year would prevent candidates from spending the invisible primary concentrating their campaigns in the region scheduled to hold the first set of primaries.

Since the 1970s, groups of states on their own have tried to develop a regional primary. Various attempts were made for a New England,

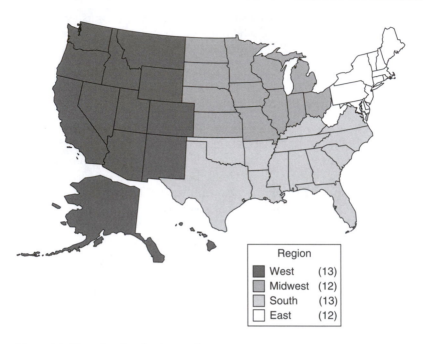

Figure 4.1 Map of regional primary plan.
Source: Regions as defined in S. 1905, 110th Congress.

Midwest, Pacific Northwest, or Rocky Mountain regional primary. While some states in these regions cooperated to coordinate their primaries or caucuses on the same date, other state legislatures failed to act. Thus, none of these areas had a full regional primary.[3] The one exception was the South which in 1988 held a regional primary on March 8 encompassing 14 southern states. The impetus for the southern regional primary was a belief that the South did not have enough clout in the selection of the presidential nominees, especially on the Democratic side. Intergovernmental regional groups, such as the Southern Legislative Conference and Southern Governors' Association, helped to coordinate the changes in state laws needed to create the southern regional primary. While the southern regional primary as a whole received considerable attention from candidates and the media, not every individual state experienced the promised benefits. As a consequence, in subsequent years southern states rescheduled their primaries or caucuses across a variety of calendar dates.[4]

Proponents of regional primaries argue the format would benefit both candidates and voters. Candidates could concentrate on campaigning in one region at a time, rather than crisscrossing the nation from east to west or north to south. With a more logical ordering to the primaries, the best candidates might be willing to run for the presidential nominations.

Candidates would have to address regional or national issues, rather than policies that appeal to only one state. Regional primaries also are seen as a way to ensure that the nomination campaign continues until more, and perhaps all, voters have had a chance to express their preferences. As a consequence, regional primaries are argued to increase turnout. The public is split on whether it would prefer such a reform to the current system. In a variety of public opinion polls from the 1980s to 2000, between 40 and 57 percent favored the regional primary format.[5]

Various arguments against the regional primary format suggest it would not live up to its promises, cost states extra money, and confuse voters. A system of four regional primaries would not guarantee that the nomination contest would continue until the last region voted. If a single candidate won the bulk of the primaries in the first two regions, or even in the first region, the other candidates would have the same incentives to withdraw from the race as they do today. The national contest could still be over before half of the nation has a chance to vote. An alternative scenario has two or three candidates splitting the vote across the different regions such that no candidate controls a majority of delegates before the convention. Today's national conventions are ill suited to engaging in the bargaining and negotiations needed to nominate a candidate, because delegates are chosen based on their loyalties to a single candidate. With a stalemate between the pledged delegate camps of competing candidates, the party elite, such as the Democratic Party's superdelegates, may have to decide the nomination.

Better candidates may not be drawn into the presidential nomination bid under the regional primary format, since candidates would still need to raise millions of dollars and make numerous campaign and fundraising visits during the invisible primary stage. Some opponents also argue that voters in the first region will continue to have more say, because candidates who feel they can do better in this first region will be more likely to run. However, to be truly viable a candidate will have to win outside his or her own region. The southern Super Tuesday in 1988 allowed then-Tennessee senator Al Gore to win delegates from the southern states, but afterwards there were no more southern primaries to help out Gore's cause. Failing to expand his base in the next round of primaries, Gore dropped out of the Democratic contest on April 21.

The regional primary format will cost states, and counties which administer most U.S. elections, money by requiring the presidential primary to be separated from primaries for other offices. One reason some states continue to hold late presidential primaries, even when they often have no say in the nomination outcome, is to coordinate the presidential primary with primaries for congressional and state offices. Every additional election costs a state millions of dollars. For example, California's early presidential primary in 2008 cost the state an extra $60 million.[6] Some small states also feel they will continue to be overlooked in a regional primary format, and thus, would not want to pay the extra cost for the separate election.

Rotating the date of regional primaries across election years may seem fair in giving each region a chance to be first. Yet, a full rotation schedule covers 16 years. The region that voted first in 2012 would not again lead off the primary season until 2028. In between, voters in this region may not have much say if candidates continue to drop out of the contest as they fall behind in voter support or financial resources. Rotating of primary dates also can be confusing for voters. Most Americans are moderate consumers of political news and frequently form habits of voting. They know that the presidential elections occur once every four years in November. If the presidential primary is held in March in one year and June another, this disrupts voters' habits and can lead to lower turnout rates.

Grouping States by Population Size: The Delaware Plan

In 1999, the Republican Party established its Advisory Commission on the Presidential Nominating Process, chaired by William E. Brock. After reviewing several proposals, the commission recommended that the 2000 Republican National Convention adopt a plan that grouped primaries by state population sizes.[7] The proposal is also called the Delaware Plan because Basil Battaglia and Richard Forsten, leaders of the Republican Party in Delaware, proposed this alternative to the Brock Commission. The plan, also, would place small states such as Delaware at the front of the calendar. The nation is divided into four groups of states. The first group, or "pod," consists of the least populous states (see Figure 4.2) plus the U.S. territories of Guam, Virgin Islands, and American Samoa. This group of states would hold their primaries or caucuses on, or any time after, the first Tuesday in March. The second group of states, being slightly larger in population sizes, would hold their events no earlier than the first Tuesday in April. The third group holds their primaries and caucuses at the beginning of May, and the states with the largest populations are assigned the first Tuesday in June. This last group of states represents more than 50 percent of the convention delegates.

The Republican National Committee at its preconvention meeting adopted the recommendation of the Brock Commission, but under Republican Party rules the plan would have to be approved by the full body at the 2000 Republican National Convention in order to be used for the 2004 Republican nomination. The intervening step would be for the Convention's Rules Committee to approve the proposal. This committee rejected the proposal, ending the Republican reform effort for that year. The rejection came as the campaign staff of George W. Bush, the soon-to-be-named Republican nominee, indicated their disapproval of the change

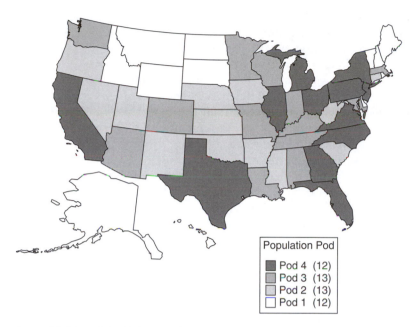

Population Pod

■ Pod 4 (12)
▨ Pod 3 (13)
▤ Pod 2 (13)
□ Pod 1 (12)

Figure 4.2 Map of the Delaware plan.
Source: Plan as defined on FairVote website.

in party rules. Such a rule change would be controversial, especially among the larger states, and the Bush organization did not want any controversy at their convention.[8]

Supporters of the Delaware Plan assert it would give more voters a say in the presidential nominations. Because 50 percent of the convention delegates are not awarded until the last group of primaries, no one candidate is likely to become the presumptive nominee before June. Concomitantly, this process would dilute the influence of the earliest events, since most of the delegates are chosen at the end of the calendar. In addition, having small states first allows for retail-style politics in the early states, where candidates conduct grassroots campaigns to meet the voters. This would allow both well-known and lesser known candidates to compete for the nomination. The Delaware Plan also eliminates the front-loading of the nomination calendar, reducing the need for the increasingly large sums of campaign funds raised during the invisible primary stage. Finally, the more gradual nomination calendar allows voters a longer time period in which to learn about and judge the merits of the various candidates.

Critics of the Delaware Plan are less sure that it would prolong the nomination contests to the last round of primaries held in June. In recent years, many candidates drop out long before even half of the delegates have been selected. The nomination process is two-tiered, with a national contest between candidates for early victories and momentum, followed by a later concentration on delegate accumulation. The first group of states will continue to eliminate many of the candidates and give other contestants more favorable odds for winning in subsequent rounds. Thus, the early states still have undue influence. In addition, these early states are small, rural, and less racially diverse than the rest of the nation. Further, despite these states being small, the grouping of 12 different states at the start of the nomination contest will still place a heavy burden on lesser known and less well-financed candidates.[9]

While both regional primaries and the Delaware Plan group states on specific dates, they do have some important differences. The Delaware Plan would not ease the travel burdens on candidates, as each primary date includes states from all areas of the country. The first pod includes western states such as Wyoming and Montana and northeastern states such as Vermont and Maine. The June group includes California and New York, as well as Texas and Michigan. Regional primaries hold out a slightly better chance of allowing candidates to concentrate campaigning in one area of the country. The Delaware Plan is more flexible on state election dates. It assigns a beginning date for each pod of states, but a state may hold a later primary if it chooses. Thus, states may conserve their financial resources by selecting a later presidential primary date to coincide with other state elections. The Delaware Plan has a fixed schedule across election years while the regional primary format rotates the schedule. With a fixed schedule, voters may develop habits of participating at certain times of the year. Yet, without rotation the same group of states always comes first.

Other Variants of Grouped Primaries

A variety of other methods have been devised to group primaries and caucuses on specific dates. Some are minor deviations from the regional primary or Delaware Plan formats. For example, the Modified Delaware Plan would allow Iowa and New Hampshire to go first, before the start of four groupings of states by population sizes.[10] The Small State First–Large State Last plan, proposed by political scientist Robert Loevy, is a precursor to the Delaware Plan, but differs by mandating the elimination of candidates at each specific round.[11] Other plans are mixtures of the population-size and regional grouping components, such as in the Ohio Plan described below. Still other variants organize states along different sets of criteria or by a random process.

The Ohio Plan

The Ohio Plan is a hybrid of the Delaware Plan and regional primaries promoted by Ohio Republican Party chairman Robert Bennett. The first group of primaries would be the small states. The other three groups would be based on approximately equal-sized regions: 1) Eastern and Midwestern states, 2) South, and 3) West. The ordering of the primaries for these three regional groups would rotate across election years. The Ohio Plan continues to allow Iowa and New Hampshire to precede the first group of small-state primaries and keeps the early slots for South Carolina and Nevada that were included in the Democratic plan for 2008. In the spring of 2008, a Republican Party panel recommended the adoption of the Ohio Plan for the 2012 Republican nomination, but a second party panel rejected the proposal before the full convention could vote on it.[12] Thus, just as in 2000, a major reform plan had been proposed but then rejected by the Republican Party.

The American Plan (also called the California Plan or the Graduated Random Presidential Primary System)

The American Plan places primaries and caucuses across 10 groups of increasing population sizes with elections held at two-week intervals. The process involves a somewhat complicated formula based on congressional districts. The first primary or group of primaries would be equal to eight congressional districts. States with eight or fewer congressional districts would be eligible for this first group. The first primary could be from a single state with eight congressional districts, such as Arizona or Minnesota, or it could be a group of states, such as Nebraska with three congressional districts paired with West Virginia with four congressional districts. The second grouping of states would be the equivalent of 16 congressional districts, the third grouping equivalent to 25 congressional districts and the tenth, and final grouping, would equal 80 congressional districts. The selection of states for each grouping would be by random draw, but the total number of congressional districts would restrict the placement of large states, such as California with 53 congressional districts, to the latter half of the nomination calendar. Advocates of this plan argue that the process would weed out uncompetitive candidates early, but still not decide the ultimate victor until the later rounds of primaries. The random selection, repeated before every nomination cycle, also would allow different states to lead off in each year.[13]

Interregional Primary Plan

The interregional primary plan begins by dividing the nation into six geographic regions, but this does not determine the date of a state's primary or caucus. Rather, a subset of states are selected from each region and assigned a specific date. States from different regions of the country would hold their primaries on the same day, thus the "interregional" name for the plan. Table 4.1 lists the regions (labeled 1 to 6) and the combination

Table 4.1 Interregional primary plan

	Region 1	Region 2	Region 3	Region 4	Region 5	Region 6
Subregion A	Maine New Hampshire Vermont	Maryland	Ohio	Texas	Virginia	California
Subregion B	Massachusetts	West Virginia	Illinois	Louisiana	North Carolina	Washington
Subregion C	Connecticut Rhode Island	Missouri	Michigan	Arkansas Oklahoma	South Carolina	Oregon
Subregion D	Delaware New Jersey	Indiana	Wisconsin	Colorado	Florida	Idaho Nevada Utah
Subregion E	New York	Kentucky	Iowa	Kansas Nebraska	Georgia	Montana North Dakota South Dakota Wyoming
Subregion F	Pennsylvania	Tennessee	Minnesota	Arizona	Alabama Mississippi	Alaska Hawaii

Source: Fair and Representative Presidential Primaries Act of 2009 (S. 1433).

of states which composed the subregions (labeled A to F). The ordering of the subregions is determined by a lottery before each election year, and the same subregion cannot go first two times in a row. If subregion C is selected by lottery as the first group, Connecticut, Rhode Island, Missouri, Michigan, Arkansas, Oklahoma, South Carolina, and Oregon would hold primaries on the second Tuesday in March. The other subregions would vote on five subsequent dates, ending with the last group of primaries held on the second Tuesday in June. An interregional primary plan has been proposed in Congress since the late 1990s. In the 111th Congress, this plan was introduced as the Fair and Representative Presidential Primaries Act of 2009. Sponsoring the legislation were Senators Bill Nelson (D-FL) and Carl Levin (D-MI).[14]

The interregional primary plan would reduce the influence of Iowa and New Hampshire by including them together with all the other states in the primary groupings. No one group of states would always lead off the election calendar. The groupings of states, however, are quite large, and if subregion A was selected as first, candidates would have to begin the campaign by simultaneously competing in Ohio, Texas, and California. Candidates would still need to amass large sums of money before the first set of primaries, and lesser known and less well-financed candidates would not be very competitive. As is true of the other rotating or lottery plans, the scheduling of the presidential primaries would be separated from primaries for other offices, costing states more money, and the ever-changing date for the presidential primary may be confusing for some voters.

One-Day National Primary

A one-day national primary seems simple. All across America, voters in every state would go to the polls on the same day to cast their ballots in either the Democratic or Republican primary. Whichever candidate won the national primary would automatically become the nominee for the party. This is how primary elections are conducted for most other offices in the United States. In a Republican primary election for a congressional seat, for example, if candidate A receives more votes than candidate B, candidate A becomes the Republican nominee. There are no complicated formulas to translate this candidate vote into convention delegates. The American public likes the simplicity of the single national presidential primary. A 1952 Gallup poll found 73 percent in favor. A 2007 poll conducted by the *New York Times* and CBS News revealed 72 percent of Americans approved of a one-day national primary.[15]

The proposal for a single national primary is one of the oldest of the proposed reforms. The first congressional proposal was introduced in 1911, the same time period when states were switching over to the direct primary for nominating candidates for statewide and congressional offices.

President Woodrow Wilson lent his support to the idea of a national presidential primary in a speech before Congress in 1913.[16] He averred that the reform was uncontroversial and should be handled promptly. Yet, the early proposals for a national presidential primary failed, as have more than 100 bills since that time.[17] The national primary reform plan stalled during the early 20th century when arguments came forward that Congress did not have the constitutional authority to change the presidential nomination process. The general reform movement of the early 20th century also came to a close with the advent of World War I.[18]

Modern arguments in support of the national presidential primary focus on its presumed simplicity and fairness. The winner of the national primary automatically becomes the party's presidential candidate. Every voter has an equal chance to influence the outcome, since all cast their ballots on the same day. No longer will the field of candidates be winnowed by earlier primaries or caucuses and no longer would the race become irrelevant before all states have a chance to hold their primary elections. A national primary would eliminate the hodgepodge of rules now used with the state-by-state primary system. A single national date, used over multiple election years, would reduce voter confusion and increase turnout.[19]

Arguments against a national primary focus on the cost of running a national campaign and the inability of lesser known candidates to compete. Even a candidate such as Barack Obama needed a sequential scheduling of multiple primary elections to gain the credibility to win the nomination. As he won more states, Obama demonstrated his ability to connect with voters and convinced more of the party's leaders to back him. A single national primary would mean campaigns composed of television advertisements and "tarmac campaigning," where candidates fly into several locations on one day making short stops and delivering the same stump speech. The retail politics of the small early primaries and caucuses would be lost. In a national campaign, candidates would focus on the large states and large urban centers where more votes could be won. Smaller and rural states could be ignored.

A single one-day national primary receives no support from the political party leaders. Party leaders fear that a factional candidate could win a national primary in which four, five, or six candidates competed. The winning candidate might be the preferred choice of 30 percent of the primary voters, but the other 70 percent might adamantly oppose this candidate. The national primary is seen as too radical by the party leaders who still see value in the national conventions for unifying the party. Moreover, a national primary would further separate candidates from the party. Some fear that a national primary would bring an end to the parties, relegating parties solely to the role of being vehicles for individual candidates to claim a label.

Alternative Mechanisms for Counting the Votes in a National Primary

A very practical problem with a national primary would be how to count the votes. Most U.S. elections use plurality voting rules. Whichever candidate receives the most votes wins. The winning candidate does not need to garner a majority of the vote, only a plurality of the vote. In most U.S. elections, plurality voting rules work because only two candidates (the Democratic candidate and the Republican candidate) have any real chance of winning the election. With only two candidates, the plurality winner is frequently a majority winner as well. Presidential nominations, however, attract a large number of candidates. In January 2008, both parties had eight candidates vying to be their presidential nominees. In a contest with five, six, or more candidates, the plurality winner may have won only 20 or 30 percent of the vote. Take the outcome of the 2008 New Hampshire primary as an example. Clinton won the Democratic contest with 39.1 percent of the vote, and John McCain won on the Republican side with 37 percent. A switch to a national presidential primary would most likely entail a switch in vote-counting rules as well.

Social scientists and mathematicians have long known that different voting rules can lead to different winning candidates. Periodically, journalists discover these facts and write articles voicing shock at such possibilities. For example, Sharon Begley in a 2008 *Newsweek* article lamented that "it is a little disturbing" for democracy that alternative voting rules can select different winners.[20] Yet, a national presidential primary would bring such issues to the forefront. Alternatives to plurality voting rules that could apply to a national presidential primary include a runoff primary, approval voting, and various methods for voters to rank candidates.

Majority Vote Rules and the Runoff Primary

Southern states do require majority victories in their primaries for state-level and congressional offices. This tradition developed in the South because after the Civil War through the 1950s, the Democratic Party was often the sole political party. The Republican Party was either very weak or nonexistent in many counties across the South. This meant that whoever won the Democratic primary would surely be elected in the fall general election. The requirement for a majority vote means that if no candidate wins 50 percent or more of the vote, another mechanism needs to come into play. In the South, a subsequent runoff primary is held a few weeks later with voters choosing between the top two candidates. Proponents of the runoff primary argue that it prevents the nomination of a fringe candidate, who could be the plurality victor in the first round. In addition, advocates speculate that a runoff may even force candidates that make it to the second round to moderate their views to broaden their base of support. Many of the recent proposals for a national presidential primary include a majority vote requirement with a subsequent runoff election if needed.[21]

Runoff primaries have their own problems. Participation in the runoff primary is frequently lower than in the first round. In parts of the country that currently use such procedures, turnout rates in the second round primary are typically one-third lower than in the first round. With a smaller turnout in the runoff primary, the composition of the electorate necessarily changes. While runoff primaries are supported as a means to avoid nominating fringe candidates, the top two finishers in the first round primary still may be factional candidates. For example, consider a candidate field with one liberal candidate, three moderate candidates, and one conservative candidate. Any one of the moderate candidates might be preferred by most of the party's voters to either the liberal or the conservative candidate. Yet, since three candidates are competing for the moderate voters, they split this vote. Meanwhile, the liberal and conservative candidates both secure enough votes to rank first and second in the initial round and those two candidates will face off against each other in the runoff portion of the primary. None of the moderate candidates makes it to the second round. In alternative scenarios, the candidate who placed first in the initial primary may not be the winner in the second round. The pattern in the southern primaries is that this occurs about one-quarter of the time.[22] Of course, a second round runoff primary will cost states more money.

Approval Voting

An alternative method for avoiding the problems in plurality voting rules is to switch to alternative vote-counting methods. One method suggested for presidential primaries is approval voting. Under approval voting, voters mark their ballots for as many candidates as they please. With four candidates' names on the ballot, a voter could vote for one, two, three, or all four candidates. The candidate with the most votes wins. Because the goal under approval voting is to accumulate as many votes as possible, even from second or third preferences, advocates for approval voting proclaim it will lead to more positive campaigning. No longer do candidates have to criticize their opponents to prevent citizens from voting for these alternative candidates. Rather candidates will stress their own positive qualities to attract more support. Advocates for approval voting also claim it would advantage moderate candidates, who could receive support from voters on both the left and right. In contrast, a candidate who stakes out a conservative position would most likely only receive votes from the most conservative voters within the party.

Proponents claim approval voting allows voters to vote sincerely rather than strategically. Strategic voting is a decision by a voter to cast a ballot for a lesser preferred candidate who has a better chance of winning an election than marking the ballot for the most preferred candidate with a lesser chance of winning the election. Strategic voting could occur in any election with more than two candidates and may be particularly relevant in presidential primaries where voters consider both their preferences for a candidate and the likelihood that this candidate could win the nomination or even the general election. Under approval voting, a citizen can vote sincerely by marking the ballot for both the most preferred candidate and the candidate with the greater electoral chances. Under approval voting a citizen also does not have to choose between candidates if they are "indifferent" between them. In this case, indifferent means a voter more or less equally likes several candidates. Under plurality voting rules, the voter would have to select only one of these candidates, but under approval voting, the voter can support all of the candidates. Because voters would not have to choose between strategic and sincere voting or make a difficult decision to pick a single candidate over a group of similar candidates, approval voting may increase turnout by making the voting decision simpler.[23]

Opponents of approval voting note that approval voting may prevent a candidate who is the first-place preference of a majority of voters from winning the election. In this scenario, a candidate who is the second-ranked preference for 70 percent of the voters would win over a candidate who is the first-ranked preference of 60 percent of the voters. Opponents also argue that strategic voting is rarely practiced to the extent that it should be a criterion for selecting an alternative voting mechanism. In a move toward a more positive campaign, voters might learn less about the candidates' issue positions. What is perceived as negative campaigning is often one candidate comparing his or her position to that of the other candidates. This helps voters to distinguish the positions of candidates. Under approval voting, in an effort to win the broadest support, candidates may merely emphasize noncontroversial issue positions and vague personal qualifications. Finally, opponents note that no local or state government election in the United States currently uses approval voting as a selection method.[24]

Instant Runoff Voting (or Hare Method)

An alternative voting process would be to have voters rank order all of the candidates. A voter would rate her or his favorite candidate as "1," the second most liked candidate as "2," the third most liked candidate as "3," and so on until the list of candidates is completed. Once voters rank order candidates, a variety of different rules exist for counting up the votes.

The most likely alternative in the United States would be instant runoff voting, since this is a reform that has been adopted at the local level in a number of communities in recent years.

Under instant runoff voting rules, step one is to count voters' first-place rankings. If one candidate wins a majority of the vote from the first-place rankings, that candidate wins. If no candidate has a majority of the vote in the first round, for the second round the candidate with the fewest first-place votes is dropped from consideration. Those voters who had supported this candidate have their votes transferred to their second ranked candidate. The totals for all the candidates are reconsidered after this transfer of votes, and if one candidate now has a majority of the vote, that candidate wins. If no candidate has a majority of the vote after the second round, the next lowest candidate is dropped, votes are transferred, and the candidates' totals tallied once again. The process continues until one candidate has a majority of the vote based on original first-place support and the support picked up in subsequent rounds after votes have been transferred.

Advocates for instant runoff rules argue that the process leads to majority support for the eventual winner, either based on voters' first-place preferences or their highest ranked preference among the most viable candidates. This would prevent factional or splinter candidates from winning the primary with a small plurality of the vote. Advocates for such a rule change also argue it would be beneficial even in a system of sequential state-by-state primaries. The media have a tendency to focus on a primary winner, regardless of overall percentage of the vote. The majority vote provision of instant runoff rules would ensure that the candidate receiving this media coverage is a candidate with more broad-based support. Instant runoff rules also would handle potential problems for the increasing number of Americans who cast early votes, usually through mailed-in absentee ballots. In a nomination process where candidates drop out of the race at different points in time, voters casting early ballots may support a candidate who drops out before the votes are actually counted. Under instant runoff, these voters' second- or third-choice candidate will receive their support. Finally, the Democratic Party already uses a form of instant runoff in its caucus setting. For a candidate to receive any delegates, he or she must have the support of a minimum of 15 percent of the caucus attendees. After an initial count, supporters of candidates who do not meet this threshold are allowed to switch their support to another candidate in a second, and final, round of voting.[25]

Critics note that ranking candidates is a more difficult task than voting for a single candidate, such as under plurality rules. A full ranking of candidates also requires a voter to make decisions between a number of similarly preferred candidates, while under approval voting the citizen simply votes equally for all. A more complicated voting process might dissuade people from voting. Counting ballots under instant runoff also is more difficult. Minneapolis recently adopted instant runoff rules for city offices, with the first use in the November 2009 elections. For many of the city offices, a majority victor was present from the first vote rankings. However, a number of lesser offices were not decided by the first-place votes and the instant runoff process was invoked. Unfortunately, computer software certified to be used with U.S. voting machines is not yet available, and election officials in Minneapolis expected it would take them a month to hand count and reallocate all the votes to obtain majority victors.[26] Of course, if instant runoff counting rules were adopted for a national primary, appropriate software would be developed. Yet, every county government in America would have to purchase this software adding to the cost of the new election. This would be a huge financial hurdle without assistance from the federal government.

Comparing Results from Different Voting Rules

Each of the vote-counting rules stresses different aspects. Plurality voting only weighs voters' first preferences and awards the victory to the candidate with the most support, even if it is not a majority vote. Approval voting weighs first and subsequent choices equally and awards the victory to the candidate with the broadest support even if that candidate may not be the first choice of most of the voters. Instant runoff voting accounts for second and third choices but only for those whose first choice is no longer viable.

Each method of counting may produce a different winner. Table 4.2 provides a hypothetical electorate composed of eight voters (Jill, Jack, Jan, Jason, Julie, John, Jessica, and Jacob) who are selecting between four candidates (A, B, C, D). The full preference rankings for each individual for the four candidates are depicted, though under certain voting rules only some of these ranking preferences are revealed. Under plurality voting

Table 4.2 Hypothetical primary election with eight voters choosing between four candidates

Candidate rankings	Voters							
	Jill	Jack	Jan	Jason	Julie	John	Jessica	Jacob
Most preferred	A	A	A	B	B	C	C	D
Second	B	B	B	C	C	B	B	C
Third	D	C	D	D	D	D	A	A
Least preferred	C	D	C	A	A	A	D	B

rules, candidate A wins as she has three first-place votes to two each for candidates B and C and only one vote for candidate D. For approval voting, voters can vote for as many candidates as they please, but let's assume voters only cast an approval vote for a candidate they rank as first or second. Under this scenario, approval voting would elect candidate B, since B received two first-place votes and five second-place votes for a total of seven votes.

The counting for instant runoff is a bit more complicated. No candidate wins on the first round, as candidate A has the most first-place votes, but this is not a majority. For the second round, candidate D is eliminated from the competition and Jacob's vote is redistributed to candidate C. Thus the vote count in the second round is three votes for candidate A, two votes for candidate B, and three votes for candidate C. Still no majority vote for any of the candidates. For round three, candidate B is eliminated and Jason's and Julie's votes are redistributed to candidate C. In round three, candidate C wins with five votes to three votes for candidate A.

The three voting rules produce three different winners. Plurality voting rules gave the election to candidate A, approval voting bestowed the election on candidate B, and instant runoff rules awarded the victory to candidate C. Mathematicians and social scientists propose a number of criteria for selecting a good voting rule. For example, the Condorcet criterion favors a voting rule that selects the same winner as would occur between pairwise comparisons between all sets of the candidates. However, a Condorcet winner does not always exist (and it does not in our hypothetical example), and the likelihood of specific voting rules selecting the Condorcet winner varies with the number of candidates. John Haskell, in his book *Fundamentally Flawed*, provides a more extensive analysis of voting rules and their application to presidential nominations.[27] The most important point for now is that switching to a single national primary would bring to the forefront questions about how to count the votes. One reform would lead to another set of problems.

Convention-Centered Plans

A final set of proposals focus on bringing the national conventions to the forefront. One plan would alter the ordering of the primaries versus the convention. Today, primaries are held in the spring to select delegates to attend the national conventions held in the late summer. The pre-primary convention plan has an earlier convention followed by primary elections. Convention delegates would make judgments on the qualifications and electability of various potential candidates, and the delegates' votes would determine which candidates' names would be placed on the ballot in a subsequent national primary. The core idea is that the convention would endorse candidates before voters would have the final say on the party's nominee. This is similar to the process used in a small number of states, where the state party convention vote leads to endorsements for candidates running in the party's primary. A second proposal would be to only hold a convention, returning to the format used in the early 20th century.

Plans differ on how convention delegates will be selected. In a pre-primary convention plan proposed by political scientists Thomas Cronin and Robert Loevy, delegates would be chosen by a process involving local caucus meetings followed by county and state conventions. This would be somewhat similar to the multi-stage process used in caucus states today. The Cronin-Loevy plan has local caucuses held nationwide on the same day in May. Potential delegates can run as "bound" to a specific candidate choice, but at least 25 percent of the state's delegates would need to be "unbound" delegates. Other proposals have the delegates for the convention composed of preexisting party officials, such as the state parties' central committees.[28]

Plans also differ on how convention votes would be translated into endorsements. Some plans would place only the top two candidates' names on the national primary ballot. Other plans would use a percentage of the convention vote, such as 25 percent, as a requirement for placement on the primary ballot. Once the conventions have chosen the names of the candidates to be placed on the primary ballot, the public selects the nominee for the party with the vote at the national primary. Whichever candidate wins the national primary automatically becomes the party's presidential nominee.

Advocates for the pre-primary convention plan argue that it would shorten the nomination campaign, increase voter attention and participation, reduce the influence of the media in declaring primary winners and losers, and increase the role for party officials and leaders. In particular, these party leaders could provide peer review of potential candidates. Party leaders and elected officials would be those who had worked with the senators and governors seeking the party's presidential nomination, and thus, would have practical information on candidates' abilities to work with Congress, build party coalitions, and make sound judgments. Finally, with a more limited set of choices, typically three or fewer, voters would be better able to learn about the issue positions and qualifications of the candidates before casting their votes in the primary election.

Opponents of the plan argue that the public expects a more dominant role in the naming of the presidential candidates. Americans would object as much to the screening of candidates by the conventions as they do to the winnowing of choices by the Iowa caucuses and New Hampshire primary. Others question whether the selection of the convention delegates, especially if chosen through the caucuses, would be any different from the current jockeying of candidates to win delegates. Certainly the national candidates would attempt to influence the choice of convention delegates at each stage of the process. Further, in order to win support at the local caucuses and state convention, candidates would have to campaign early and often in the states.[29]

Pathways to Reform

As is obvious from the above discussion, numerous ideas exist for improving the presidential nomination process. Why then have none been put into place? Any dramatic policy change is difficult. Most changes in policies, whether they are those of the government or of organizations such as the political parties, are incremental—small changes to existing practices. Thus, in recent years the two parties have altered the starting date for the primary calendar, gradually moving it forward to February 1. In contrast, the Republican Party in 2000 failed to adopt the major reformatting of the primary calendar as presented by the Delaware Plan. Reforms could be enacted by three separate groups: from Congress, from the national parties, or from state governments.

Reform through Congressional Action

One possible way to reform the presidential primary system is through Congress passing a law. As noted above, numerous bills have been introduced for a national primary, regional primaries, and interregional primaries. As is the case with most legislation introduced into Congress, more often than not these bills died without even receiving a hearing in one of the congressional committees. After all, 90 percent of legislation dies in this fashion. Added to normal difficulties of getting legislation heard is the question of whether Congress has the constitutional authority to alter presidential nomination rules. This question of constitutionality is what stalled the early 20th-century attempts to adopt a national presidential primary.

The constitutionality argument centers on different wordings for federal regulation of congressional elections versus presidential elections. For congressional elections, the Constitution allows Congress to regulate the "times, places, and manner" of holding these elections. For presidential elections, the Constitution only mentions Congress regulating the date for choosing the electors for the Electoral College, leaving the manner of selecting these electors up to the states. Some scholars, such as William Mayer and Andrew Busch, argue that this different wording limits the ability of Congress to establish rules for presidential nominations. In contrast, Richard Hasen argues that the Constitution would allow Congress to set the dates for presidential primaries under a necessary and proper clause extension of setting the date for the presidential election.

However, Hasen does question whether Congress could prescribe other rules for the presidential primaries, such as requiring proportional representation delegate allocation rules.[30]

Besides the question over the meaning of the language in the Constitution, arguments against congressional action focus on the rights of states to regulate elections and the rights of parties to create their own nomination procedures. Mayer and Busch also argue that federal law would produce a more rigid set of rules for primaries that would be more difficult to modify if times changed. Of course, a constitutional amendment could be passed to create a national primary or adopt one of the plans that group states, but this would require a two-thirds vote in the House and the Senate and the approval of three-fourths of the states.

Reform Sponsored by the National Parties

The political parties have the right to reform their presidential nomination processes. Indeed, they have done so in the past as early as the 1830s when they switched from congressional caucuses to national conventions. Further, a variety of U.S. Supreme Court rulings from the 1970s through 2000 have focused on the parties' First Amendment right of association. In rulings from *Cousins v. Wigoda* (1974) and *Democratic Party v. Wisconsin* (1981), the Supreme Court validated the efforts of the national Democratic Party to enforce its rules for delegate selection on state parties and state governments. In *Tashjian v. Republican Party of Connecticut* (1986) and *California Democratic Party v. Jones* (2000), the Supreme Court granted state parties the right to determine who votes in their primaries.[31] Thus, the national parties have the constitutional right to formulate their own rules for selection of delegates to the national conventions and in the process make rules for presidential primaries and caucuses.

The first step toward reforms originating from the political parties is to obtain consensus among the parties' leaders. A party-sponsored reform commission or a preexisting party organization, such as the Democratic or Republican National Committees, would need to agree on a new set of rules. Such consensus may be hard to obtain, as different geographical or ideological factions of the parties have different perspectives on how new rules will affect their interests. Even when the party leaders find agreement among themselves, they face the additional hurdle of trying to obtain compliance with any rules they do change. In a January 2008 meeting of the Republican National Committee, National Committeeman Bob Kjellander expressed such frustration: "We can, in a vacuum in this room, vote out a plan. But getting 50 state legislatures to follow it is a whole other question."[32] In recent years, both parties have tried to coax state parties to hold later primaries by awarding additional delegates and punished states with too early dates by withholding delegates. Neither tactic has worked. Further, a comprehensive plan, such as a national primary, would require coordination across the Democratic and Republican parties. In most years, the party winning the election has little incentive for major reform, since existing rules produced a winning presidential candidate.

Nevertheless, both parties created reform commissions to possibly rewrite the rules for the 2012 nominations. The Democratic Party created its Change Commission to investigate questions involving the primary and caucus calendar, the role of superdelegates, and the format for caucuses. The Change Commission made three recommendations in December 2009. First, they proposed that the start of the nomination calendar be pushed back to March, with exceptions for Iowa, New Hampshire, Nevada and South Carolina. Incentives would be offered to encourage other states to form regional clusters or to select later primary dates. Second, the commission recommended keeping superdelegates but stripping them of their independent voice. Instead, superdelegates would be bound by the results of their states' primary or caucus. Finally, the commission recommended that the party develop a list of "best practices" for caucuses. These commission recommendations were forwarded to the Democratic National Committee (DNC)'s Rules and Bylaws Committee, with any final action to be taken by the full membership of the DNC. The Republican Party established the Temporary Delegate Selection Committee, with any of its recommendations requiring a two-thirds vote by the Republican National Committee at its summer 2010 meeting.[33]

The Role of the States

As indicated by Mr. Kjellander's statement, the states, and in particular the state legislatures, would need to implement any dramatic change in the primary calendar. State legislatures set the dates for elections in their states and establish other election rules. In some cases, state parties organize the procedures for selecting delegates to the national conventions. This most typically occurs in the caucus states, but occasionally, a state party will sponsor a presidential primary. For example, the New Mexico Democratic Party sponsored its own primary on Super Duper Tuesday in 2008 rather than using the state-sponsored primary set for June 3.

State legislators have their own sets of goals when scheduling presidential primaries. In some cases, state legislators do want more clout for their state in the presidential nomination process. Thus, they pass new state laws to change the date of a primary or switch from the caucus format to a primary. Other state legislators focus on the cost of holding a separate presidential primary and instead coordinate the presidential primary with congressional primaries on a late spring date. State legislators generally do not want to move their own primaries forward into early March or

February, as they view these dates as too early to start their own reelection campaigns. State finances also play a role in state legislature decisions. In 2004, a handful of states canceled presidential primaries in face of state budget shortfalls.

Partisan politics also can play a role. In Arizona, the 1996 presidential primary was scheduled for February 27, a date favored by the Republican governor and Republican-controlled legislature. This date, however, was too early under national Democratic Party rules. The Republican Party used the state-sponsored primary while the Arizona Democratic Party in 1996 and 2000 was forced to schedule, and pay for, its own caucuses held in March. Before the 2004 election, the Republican majority in the Arizona legislature voted to cancel the presidential primary to save the state $3 million. Besides, President George W. Bush would be renominated in that year, making the Republican primary superfluous. However, the Democratic race was wide open and new Democratic rules for 2004 allowed a February primary. Thus, Arizona's Democratic governor, Janet Napolitano, vetoed the legislation.[34] State partisan politics often spills over into debates on presidential nomination laws.

Rescuing the Matching Funds System

Besides reform plans that address problems with the primary and caucus election calendar, a second venue for possible reform would be to rescue the matching fund system in place since the early 1970s. As discussed in Chapter 2, campaign finance laws provide two places in which public (i.e., government) funding occurs in presidential campaigns. For the fall presidential election, the major party candidates receive a set amount of money for their campaigns from the federal government. In 2008, this total was $84 million. Barack Obama was the first candidate to reject the government funds for the general election campaign. During the nomination phase, a candidate qualifies for federal matching funds by raising $100,000 in contributions of $250 or less spread out across 20 states. Once a candidate raises this sum of money, contribution amounts under $250 are matched by government funds dollar for dollar. Since the late 1990s, more and more candidates have rejected the matching fund system for the nomination phase. They do so because a candidate accepting matching funds is limited in the amount of money that can be spent in any one state and in the total amount spent on the entire campaign. Thus, candidates such as George Bush in 2000, John Kerry in 2004, and Hillary Clinton, Barack Obama, and John McCain in 2008 did not participate in the matching fund system, relying solely on individual contributions and surpassing the spending limits attached to the matching funds.

The matching fund system was developed to encourage candidates to raise funds in small sums of money. This would prevent candidates from relying on large contributions from a small segment of wealthier American donors. Matching funds also did not apply to contributions from interest groups in the form of political action committee (PAC) contributions. As a result, interest group money accounts for less than 5 percent of the funds raised in presidential nomination campaigns. The matching fund system also allowed more candidates to compete for the nomination bid, by providing lesser known candidates financial assistance in accumulating the money needed to compete with better known candidates.

In order to save the federal matching fund system, the amount of money available to candidates would need to be raised significantly to make it more attractive to candidates. The current system is a one-for-one match. This might have to be raised to a four-to-one or six-to-one match. Under the latter, a $250 contribution from an individual would be worth $1,750 to the campaign. Yet, this change in the matching fund formula would produce a second problem. Where would this money come from? To date, the government money for the presidential campaigns comes from a $3 check-off on the federal income tax form. Not many Americans are contributing to this fund even though it does not raise their tax burden. As a result, in years such as 2004 the presidential campaign fund (that pays for both the primary matching fund and the general election payments) was nearly bankrupt. If more Americans could not be convinced to contribute to the presidential campaign funds, money would have to be taken from the government's general fund. Given the yearly deficits that already exist in the federal government's budget, allocating a portion of the money to presidential elections may not be a likely prospect. Still, Congress has the authority to change the campaign finance law if it decides to do so.

The spending limits attached to the acceptance of matching funds would have to be increased, as well. Under the interpretations of the U.S. Supreme Court, spending limits can only be imposed on candidates by a voluntary method. Thus, spending limits can be a condition for accepting government money for a campaign, but a campaign that does not accept government funds cannot be required to abide by spending limits. In the primaries, spending limits exist for individual states (based on population size) and for the entire campaign. The spending limit for Iowa in 2008 for those accepting the federal matching funds was $1.5 million, but Clinton spent $4.6 million and Obama doled out $5.8 million. In 2008, the national spending limit was $42 million. Obama raised more than $400 million during the primary phase of the campaign, and the totals for Clinton and McCain were over $200 million.[35] Spending limits would have to be increased substantially to make acceptance of federal matching funds attractive. On the other hand, spending limits could be dropped for all candidates, even for those who accept matching funds.

Some argue that the matching fund system is no longer needed, because the internet allows candidates to raise large sums of money from small contributions. Small contributions can and do come in via the internet. In 2008, 50 percent of Obama's contributions during the primary phase were in sums of $200 or less. Clinton and McCain received approximately one-third of their contributions from small contributions. Yet, two factors need to be considered. First, some of the small contributions come from individuals who make repeated contributions. Thus, if Obama's contributions are categorized by individual donors, rather than donation size, 27 percent came from individuals contributing less than $200, 26 percent from sums over $200 and less than $1,000, and 47 percent from large contributions. The second factor is that early money contributed to a candidate's campaign, during the first months of the invisible primary, tends to be in large contributions. Only after a candidate becomes known will individuals seek out a website in order to make a contribution.[36]

A final component of the presidential campaign finance law is that candidates may continue to spend as much of their own money on the campaign as they see fit. This also is the result of U.S. Supreme Court rulings on campaign finance. The Court views campaign contributions as a form of free speech that cannot be restricted except for another overriding governmental concern.[37] Contributions to candidates from other individuals and interest groups can be limited to avoid the appearance of favoritism or bribery. This would not be relevant for a candidate's own money. Thus, in 1996 and 2000, Forbes relied on his own fortune to fund his two tries for the Republican nomination. Clinton in 2008 loaned her campaign $11.4 million dollars, most of which was not repaid and thus became a direct contribution. Romney contributed more than $45 million to his campaign, equal to 44 percent of his total.[38] Congress attempted to address concerns over wealthy candidates spending their own money when they allowed congressional candidates facing such candidates to raise contributions in larger sums. However, the U.S. Supreme Court overturned this law.[39] Thus, wealthy candidates willing to spend their own money will continue to be able to do so. However, candidates relying on their own personal wealth often lose the elections, perhaps because a lack of contributions from others signals a lack of public support.

Predicting the Consequences of Reform

Even if a new set of reforms is successfully passed, predicting the outcome of those reforms is difficult. Presidential nomination politics is complicated, involving more than laws or party rules. Actions by the candidates, campaign activists and donors, campaign professionals, the media, and the American voter will jointly determine the structure of any new system of presidential nominations. Members of these groups have their own priorities, goals, and patterns of behavior. Each will make decisions on its own without coordinating with or anticipating the behavior of other actors.

The new nomination system may come close to the goals of the reformers, or it may deviate significantly from what they intended.

Unintended consequences have arisen from past reforms, often building over several election cycles. When the Democratic Party's McGovern-Fraser Commission issued new rules for its 1972 convention, it wanted to make the delegate selection process fairer. The commissioners did not necessarily intend to favor the creation of more presidential primaries, but that was one of the consequences. The new system placed a premium on running in all of the primaries and winning early to enhance a candidate's chances of winning in subsequent primaries. Not all candidates understood the new rules, allowing outsider candidates such as George McGovern and Jimmy Carter to win the 1972 and 1976 Democratic nominations. By 1980, most of the candidates understood the new rules, and the early primaries and the Iowa caucuses took on extra significance. The failure of Edward Kennedy in 1980 and Gary Hart in 1984 to unseat at the convention the candidates leading in delegates at the end of the primaries (i.e., Carter and Mondale) led future candidates to withdraw earlier from the nomination races when they fell behind in primary victories or delegate totals. Shorter candidacies led to an even greater push for states to adopt early primary dates to allow their citizens to have a say on the presidential nominations. Thus, states began a battle to be one of the first to hold a primary, producing an increasingly front-loaded nomination calendar.

Advocates of a single national primary or one of the plans to group primaries by region or population size all have good reasons to favor their preferred set of reforms. They make arguments about rationalizing the nomination calendar and ensuring fairness across the states. They predict that voter participation will increase. Yet, we cannot know if any of these will hold true. Candidates will try to use the new rules to their best advantage. Activists and donors will continue to evaluate the candidates before regular voters develop an interest in the campaign. The media will still evaluate the performance of the candidates before, during, and after the primaries. New technologies will change the way candidates communicate and raise funds, and allow citizens to promote their own interpretation of candidate stances and performances. New rules can appear to be rationalizing the presidential nomination process, but the resulting politics is hard to predict.

Chapter 5

Oddities, Biases, and Strengths of U.S. Presidential Nomination Politics

The presidential nomination process is far from perfect. It is an odd combination of primary elections, local caucuses, and national conventions. Democrats use one set of rules, while the Republican Party uses a variety of other rules. In addition, the process and rules vary across the 50 states and by election year. This nomination system includes a number of biases, as well. Some biases are connected to the election calendar; others are linked to party rules on delegate distribution and allocation. Some biases advantage a few states over the others; others appear to advantage specific candidates. Meanwhile, the strengths of the current system are its flexibility and the opportunity for a variety of voices from within the party to be heard. When most elements of the party rally around a single candidate, the process produces a nominee in a short period of time. In other years, nomination contests are prolonged as no one candidate appeals to all components of the party.

In this final chapter, the oddities, biases, and strengths in early 21st-century American presidential nomination politics will be recapped. However, these three characteristics are not unique to the most recent nomination era. In the 1830s, the parties switched from congressional caucuses to national conventions to nominate presidential candidates because conventions were viewed as more representative and fairer. Yet, at national conventions before the Civil War some states went unrepresented while other states sent competing or oversized delegations, candidates' supporters sought rules that advantaged their favorites, and deadlocked conventions turned to dark horse candidates.[1] In the mid-20th century, the delegate selection process was even more esoteric than today, with only a handful of states holding presidential primaries. The remaining states relied on unpublicized caucuses, direct selection of delegates by party officials, or other methods with little public input.[2] Party reforms from the 1970s produced greater fairness in delegate selection, but subsequent trends toward front-loading and early candidate withdrawals created their own problems. The presidential nomination system keeps evolving, producing an odd and biased combination of old and new rules.

Oddities in U.S. Presidential Nomination Politics

The American way of nominating presidents appears odd to citizens of most other democratic countries. In parliamentary democracies, which are common in Europe, a prime minister is selected from the majority party, or a coalition of parties, that controls the legislative branch. Voters in the general election mark their ballots for a party or for a member of the parliament. Voters do not directly cast ballots for the prime minister. Instead, candidates for prime minister are the leaders of the various political parties. These individuals most often have considerable governmental service, either in parliament or in another high elective office. The parties' candidates for prime minister are selected by the party leadership and in some cases, in consultation with dues-paying members of the party. Peer review is a strong element to many of these procedures. In many cases, the parties' prime minister candidates are the same individuals held over from one election to the next.

The extended U.S. presidential election cycle also is odd in comparison to other democratic countries. Candidates seeking either the Democratic or Republican Party's presidential nomination often begin to test the waters two or three years before the next election. These candidates make trips to Iowa and New Hampshire and begin to court the support of party activists and donors. In parliamentary democracies, short campaigns are the norm. Elections are not held on a set schedule, such as the four-year presidential election cycle in the United States. Elections are called at any point within a specific period of time, perhaps four to five years, and can be brought on by a crisis in the government. With no set election cycle, candidates cannot engage in "invisible primary" activities.

Parliamentary democracies produce unified governments, e.g., the same party controls both the legislative and executive branches, and the executive branch is headed by an experienced party leader. If the United States had maintained the congressional caucus system for presidential nominations, in place prior to 1830, it would have a nomination process more similar to that in parliamentary democracies. The parties' members in Congress would select the presidential nominees. Yet, nominations by congressional caucus were eliminated, in part, for violating the separation of powers between the legislative and executive branches as established by the U.S. Constitution.

In presidential systems, more common in Latin America, individuals run for the post as the country's chief executive. Yet, even in these cases, candidates are more often chosen by party leaders or by rules drawn up by the political parties. U.S. parties are more heavily regulated by government laws than parties in other countries. As a result, parties in other countries may change their nomination processes more frequently, and the parties within one country may each use different methods for nominations.

A trend toward greater use of primary elections is occurring, though the use of primaries in other countries is still rare. Further, two differences exist between these primaries and those used in the United States. First, primary participation is often limited to dues-paying or other well-defined party members. Second, most of the parties use a single nationwide primary election to nominate their presidential candidates.[3]

The presidential nomination process is an oddity within the context of U.S. politics, as well. Nominations for most elective offices, such as senators or governors, are through the direct primary. Whichever candidate wins a direct primary election automatically becomes the party's nominee. This too would be the method for presidential nominations if the United States switched to a national presidential primary, though this prospect seems unlikely. Rather, some combination of caucuses and primaries scattered across the 50 states is used to select delegates to attend a national party convention. Primary victories and the accumulation of convention delegates determine the outcome of the nomination.

Presidential primaries and caucuses on the Democratic side, and a few in the Republican Party as well, are a rare usage of proportional representation rules in the United States. Proportional representation is a common election rule in other democracies. Voters cast their ballots for their preferred party, and the distribution of seats in the legislature is determined according to this vote. A party that wins 40 percent of the votes receives 40 percent of the legislative seats. In U.S. presidential nominations, a candidate who receives 40 percent of the Democratic primary vote in a state is awarded 40 percent of the state's national party convention delegate total. This use of proportional representation rules was fully adopted by the Democrats in the 1990s as a fairer method for distributing convention delegates to candidates. Yet as indicated in Chapter 3, proportional representation rules have been controversial and can produce different results than other methods for allocating convention delegates. Rules on who can vote in the primaries also are an oddity, though these rules extend to all types of primaries in the United States. In some states, only those registered as partisans are allowed to vote in the primaries; in other states, anyone can vote in either party's primary; and in the remaining states, only independents have a choice between the Republican or Democratic primary while partisans are confined to their own party's primary.

Finally, presidential elections and nominations are odd within the U.S. context in that public (e.g., government) funds are used to finance these elections. During the primary phase, candidates may qualify for a matching fund system where the government matches one-for-one small donations to the presidential contenders. Through the 1990s, candidates seeking the presidential nominations gathered 60 percent of their funds from individual contributions and one-third from the government matching fund system.[4] In the general election, the government provides the two major parties' presidential candidates with a lump sum of money for their fall campaigns. In other races for federal offices (i.e., House of Representatives and Senate), federal law limits the amount of contributions from individuals and PACs, but does not provide any government subsidies to these candidates. By 2008, both the primary and general election public funding systems were in jeopardy as fewer candidates participated. So this oddity of presidential election politics may be less prevalent in the future.

Biases in U.S. Presidential Nomination Politics

All election systems are biased. No one set of rules is the fairest. Most Americans are comfortable with the way we elect candidates for legislative posts: single-member districts with plurality election rules. States are divided into a number of legislative districts, and the candidate in each district that receives the most votes, whether it is a majority or not, is elected. Yet, this set of election rules significantly restricts the number of viable parties in the United States to only two. Other democracies have three, four, or five major political parties because they have different voting rules, such as proportional representation or majority vote requirements. In fact, this regularity between election rules and the number of competitive parties is so well established it has a particular name: Duverger's law, after the French social scientist who noted the patterns in the 1950s.[5]

Any system of sequentially scheduled primaries and caucuses will contain biases. States that have their elections at the beginning of the calendar will be perceived as having more influence than states with later dates. Certainly, voters in the early primary and caucus states winnow the field of candidates. Candidates who fail to place first, second, or third in one of the early events drop out of the contests. Yet, in many cases, the early winnowing is of candidates who failed to raise sufficient funds, which is an indicator of lack of widespread support among the party's activists. Other early casualties may not have found a voice that resonates with voters. More crucial decisions come later in the primary calendar, when the remaining stronger candidates compete against one another. This ultimate decision, however, may come before the last round of primaries and caucuses, leaving citizens in those states with no formal voice.

The primary and caucus calendars used in 2000–2008 resulted from efforts by states to maintain, create, or counter biases. These attempts were based on the assumption that holding an early nominating event brings more clout to a state. New Hampshire and Iowa attained their spots at the front of the line by accident, but they fiercely protect these spots from encroachment by other states. In 2008, these efforts went so far that the Iowa caucuses were scheduled for January 3, leaving candidates contemplating the best way to campaign over the holidays. Other states want to get to the front of the line, as well. California, which traditionally held its presidential primary at the beginning of June, increasingly moved its primary date forward over a numbers of years in search of more clout. In 2008, California moved to the first Tuesday in February, along with 20 other states, to create Super Duper Tuesday. Michigan and Florida unhappy with their positions selected even earlier dates which were outside of the framework of both national parties, leading to the showdown over delegates. Even reform movements played into this frontloading. In 1988 when the southern states put together their regional primary, they placed it early on the nomination calendar. This led to some of the earliest frontloading of the nomination calendar. Thus, any sequential primary calendar leads to perceived, and actual, biases.

Many Americans might favor a presidential nomination system where all voters have a chance to indicate their candidate preferences and in which the choice involves a number of presidential contenders. Yet, these two goals may be contradictory. The best way to guarantee that all voters have an equal voice is to hold a national primary, but a national primary would most likely limit the electoral choices to well-known and well-financed candidates. Of course, even a sequential calendar, especially one that is front-loaded, gives an advantage to better known and better financed candidates. Sequential primary elections means that in some years, and maybe even in many years, the nomination contest will be over before all states have held their primaries. The role of the American citizen, however, is not limited to their formal voice in casting ballots. The internet has made it easier for citizens to "vote" by contributing money, participating in social networking sites, or uploading their own video or text content.

Beyond biases connected to the nomination calendar, Chapter 3 noted controversies surrounding delegate allocations across the states and the distribution of delegates to candidates based on the primary results. The caucus format and the role of the Democratic Party's superdelegates also drew criticism during the 2008 campaign. Concerns over potential biases connected to who votes in primaries also reoccur periodically. Are primary voters too ideologically extreme? Do crossover voters distort the party's ability to nominate its own candidate or do such voters enhance the chances of selecting a nominee more widely acceptable to independent voters? Each set of party rules or state laws has consequences, and for some observers, these consequences will appear to be biased.

Perceived and actual biases in presidential nomination practices arise from sources other than party rules and state laws. A common concern is with the role and influence of the media. Well documented is that the media cover primary elections, and most other elections as well, as horse races. Reports focus on poll numbers, campaign funds raised, and disputes within campaign staffs. The media view these types of information as new and noteworthy and more likely to grab the attention of their audience. Even when coverage turns more directly to the candidates, the media pay more attention to candidates' personalities than issue positions. Only if a candidate adopts a new issue position or contradicts an older one is an issue considered newsworthy. But such changes are rare. With a steady stream of horse-race and personality coverage, potential voters often feel that they are short changed, not receiving the information they need to make an informed choice.

Some argue that the media are too influential in presidential nomination politics. The importance of Iowa and New Hampshire is enhanced because the media pay so much attention to these two opening events. Throughout the nomination phase, the media set expectations for how well candidates should do in an upcoming primary or caucus and subsequently interpret the outcome of the primary based on these expectations. Media coverage is part of the momentum process, with increased coverage for candidates doing well in the primary contests. Frontrunners, on the other hand, receive more critical coverage, in part because the media are relaying criticisms of the frontrunner lodged by other candidates.[6]

Another concern is whether the media are biased in favor of or against specific candidates. John McCain is an interesting example. In 2000, a common perception was that McCain received favorable coverage from the mainstream media. McCain was unusually accessible to the press, and McCain's upset victory in New Hampshire was the type of drama the media like to cover. In addition, McCain had a compelling personal story as a former prisoner of war. However, when Phillip Paolino and Daron Shaw compared the coverage of Bush and McCain from the invisible primary phase through the initial contests, they found Bush advantaged in the amount and positivity of media coverage in the earliest reports but with Bush and McCain tied in coverage after New Hampshire.[7] McCain received better coverage than the other 2008 Republican challengers, but no better coverage than Bush or momentum candidates in previous years. On the other hand, in 2008 McCain received more negative coverage from the mainstream media during the invisible primary stage when his campaign was faltering, garnered favorable coverage as he won in New Hampshire, and then faded from the headlines after winning the Republican nomination. Instead, the media turned their attention to the close battle between Clinton and Obama.[8] In both 2000 and 2008, McCain came under heavy criticism from radio talk show hosts, though the influence of these pundits is heavily debated.[9] Thus, a mixed bag of evidence exists for media bias in coverage of specific presidential contenders.

Candidates, too, try to shape the system to their own best advantages. Thus, candidates, or their supporters, attempt to create favorable bias. Some candidates actively pursue rule changes. Jesse Jackson's complaints on how alternative delegate distribution rules disadvantaged his campaigns in 1984 and 1988 were one of the factors that led the Democratic Party to ultimately settle on proportional representation rules in the early 1990s. Other candidates changed campaign techniques. Jimmy Carter in 1976 led the way to a campaign strategy that focuses on early victories in Iowa and New Hampshire to create momentum and a subsequent strategy of competing in all the remaining primaries to gain the number of delegates needed to secure the nomination. Other candidates altered strategies for raising campaign funds. Ronald Reagan perfected using direct mail in the 1970s and 1980s to raise small sums of money from a large number of people. Other candidates, such as George H. W. Bush, learned how to put together networks of donors contributing the maximum allowable amounts. John McCain in 2000 opened the door to raising funds via the internet. In 2004, Dean laid the path to using social networking technology to mobilize supporters.[10] The first candidate to adopt or perfect a technique has an edge, though others will soon follow. Nevertheless, candidates strive for rules and strategies that will be to their own advantage.

Strengths of U.S. Presidential Nomination Politics

While the presidential primaries are imperfect, they do have many good qualities. The nomination system allows for multiple voices to be heard. Many average Americans vote when faced with an interesting primary contest. More consistently, activists and campaign donors scrutinize candidates during the invisible primary stage. Party officials and elected officials endorse candidates, even if they are not superdelegates. Political pundits chime in as well. And every year, a number of current or past senators and governors try their hand at winning their party's presidential bid. While the nomination process is a complicated amalgamation of primaries, caucuses, rules, and laws, flexibility exists. In many years, intra-party consensus develops and brings the race to a quick close. In other years, the process is extended as the party more slowly makes up its collective mind.

For most of the 20th century, U.S. political parties were described by political scientists as composed of three distinctive parts.[11] The first part was the formal party organization, made up of party officers, such as the chairs of the national or state organizations, and activists who supported the parties with their donations and volunteered time. The second part of the party was the party in government, those individuals who were elected to public office under the party's label. The third element of the party was the party in the electorate—the average voter who saw themselves as a Democrat or Republican.

More recently, political scientists are taking a newer view of the structure of American political parties. Parties are viewed as social networks.

Party officials, government officials, and voters are still part of these social networks, but also included are interest groups, social movements, political consultants, donors and activists, and partisan-leaning elements of the media. These social-network political parties have multiple components, sometimes competing voices, and overlapping memberships with other political groups. Democratic activists may also be members of traditionally Democratic groups, such as labor unions; issue-oriented groups, such as NARAL; or recently formed groups, such as MoveOn. The Republican Party intersects with religious conservatives concerned about abortion and gay marriage, economic conservatives who favor lower taxes and less government regulation of business, and foreign policy conservatives who favor a stronger military.[12] The elements of the partisan social networks are not constant over time. New issues bring out new activists. Candidates also can mobilize new activists. Many of today's Republican activists trace their involvement to support for Ronald Reagan in the 1970s and 1980s. Ronald Reagan, in turn, moved to the national political stage with a nomination speech for Barry Goldwater in 1964.

The presidential nominating system has a voice or role for each element of the party. Yet, the influence of each group is not the same, and the role of various components may change over different election years. In 2000 on the Republican side, many of the party's major donors lined up behind George W. Bush during the invisible primary. With an ample war chest, Bush opted out of the government matching fund system and the accompanying limits of spending. In 2008, no one candidate seemed to be able to unite the social, economic, and military conservative activists of the Republican Party. Only after McCain won important early primaries, and other candidates engaged in faulty strategies, did a majority of Republicans rally behind McCain. Meanwhile, the Democratic Party had its longest race since 1984, between two strong candidates both with their own group of fervent supporters. Yet, for most Democrats the outcome was not divisive. Clinton endorsing Obama helped heal lingering resentments over perceived biases in delegate distribution decisions and the caucus process. In addition, the issue distinctions between Clinton and Obama were not that great. Further because of their strong disapproval of the Bush presidency, many Democratic voters would prefer any of their party's potential nominees over the Republican candidate.

Political parties often experience a tension between two types of members: purists and pragmatists (sometimes called amateurs and professionals). Purists care deeply about specific issues and support candidates who adopt these same issue positions. Purists are seen as unwilling to compromise on these issues in order to win elections. Further, they often assume that such compromises are unnecessary because purists believe they can convince the American public to join them in these issue preferences. Meanwhile, pragmatists have more loyalty to the party as an organization and more willingness to make compromises in order to win elections. The origin of the conflict between purists and pragmatists dates back to the end of World War II.[13] The decline of political patronage eliminated some of the pragmatists from the political parties. A wealthier and better educated public brought in more issue activists. Descriptions of the relative strength of purists versus professionals vary across different presidential nomination contests. Further, sometimes it is the Democratic Party that is described as experiencing more of this conflict, and at other times, it is the Republican Party.

How much tension exists within a party, whether between purists and pragmatists, different elements of the social network, or competing strong-willed candidates, will influence the level of conflict generated by any presidential nomination process. A unified party should experience quick, uneventful nominations. A factionalized party will struggle through the nomination, whether it is in a primary-dominated process or in a national convention. Thus, presidential nomination politics for Republicans in 1976 and Democrats in 1984 continued up to the conventions. In 1924, the Democratic national convention lasted 17 days and 108 ballots before reaching a decision. Recent depictions of the Democratic and Republican parties paint them as more internally cohesive and externally polarized. Thus, political conflict may be less evident within each party and more prevalent between the two. Candidates running for a party's presidential nomination mostly present nuanced differences in issue positions, though these details are important to some purists. Yet, for many voters and activists their party's winning candidate will be "close enough" on the issues in comparison to the opposition party's nominee.

Nominating Presidents in a System with Oddities, Biases, and Strengths

Presidential nominations are a political process. Politics is neither efficient nor rational. The rules that govern a political process are inherently biased to some extent, though of course, some rules may be more biased than others. The rules, also, are internal to the political process in that rules can be, and are, changed. The U.S. presidential nomination process has evolved from nominations by the parties inside of Congress, through conventions dominated by party professionals, to convention delegates selected by the public. These nomination changes reflect changes in the parties. American political parties began as coalitions of elites inside Congress. As states enfranchised more white male voters, the parties grew into mass-based organizations centering on state politics. A national convention brought together these state parties to nominate an attractive top-of-the-ticket presidential nominee. As state party bosses waned, national interest groups emerged, and an activist public evolved, nomination politics moved to an electorally based mechanism. Voters' ballot results would produce running tallies of candidates' delegate totals.

The imperfect primaries will continue to be the center of political debates. Jonathan Alter in a 2009 *Newsweek* article averred that "The American primary system allows a handful of activists to determine who runs the country."[14] Alter was referring to all primaries, not just presidential primaries, but he voiced a common complaint that issue activists are pulling both parties to the extremes. Primary elections, especially closed primaries, Alter argues, lead to a biased electorate that nominates extremist candidates. Alternatively, George F. Will in his 2007 *Newsweek* column looked at the upcoming 2008 presidential primary calendar and defended the system as "Messy, But Not a Mess."[15] He concluded that the process sufficiently reveals the traits and characteristics of the presidential nominee seekers. Other editorial writers disagree, and many in late 2007 and early 2008 called for regional primaries or other reforms.

The imperfect primaries will continue to evolve, sometimes by leaps, sometimes by increments. The sources of these transformations may be from modifications in party rules and state laws or they may be from changes in candidate strategies and campaign technology. The outcome of any of these changes will be hard to predict, as the parties are interwoven networks of diverse elements. How one element reacts to a change in the presidential nomination process may determine the responses of other segments of the political parties. Any new procedure will be added on top of old elements. The resulting system will have its own merits but also its own biases.

Notes

1 Happenstance and Reforms

1 Jules Witcover, "The McCain Dilemma," *Salt Lake City Tribune*, July 13, 2007; "Back from the Dead," *Newsweek*, November 17, 2008, 50–58.
2 "How He Did It," *Newsweek*, November 17, 2008, 38–49.
3 Primary advertising expenditures are in Pennsylvania from January 1, 2007 to June 4, 2008 as measured by TNS Media Intelligence/Campaign Media Analysis Group and posted on CNN webpages, http://www.cnn.com/ELECTION/2008/map/ad.spending/ (accessed June 10, 2008).
4 In general, the Republican Party allocated three unpledged slots per state: the state's two Republican National Committee members and the state party chair. Some states choose to send more of their allocated delegates as unpledged delegates. The New York delegation percent is calculated over the potential pledged delegate total, using only the first criterion of three delegates per state as the unpledged total.
5 Kevin J. Coleman, *Presidential Nominating Process: Current Issues*, CRS Report for Congress, RL34222, April 11, 2008, http://fpc.state.gov/documents/organization/106173.pdf (accessed March 5, 2010).
6 "A Helter-Skelter Primary System," *The Oregonian*, January 2, 2008; "Primary Train Wreck," *Boston Globe*, January 17, 2008; "Let it Start Now," *New York Times*, January 4, 2008; "Let's Switch to Regional Primaries," *Columbus Dispatch*, January 6, 2008; "Democrats' Chaotic Caucus Begs for Regional Reform," *Santa Fe New Mexican*, February 7, 2008; "Chaotic Primary System Needs Reform," *Kansas City Star*, February 7, 2008; and "Super, But Still Flawed: Early Vote Worked for California, but ...," *Sacramento Bee*, February 7, 2008.
7 George F. Will, "Messy, But Not a Mess," *Newsweek*, November 5, 2007, 72.
8 Information on the 1860 convention is from R. Craig Sautter and Edward M. Burke, *Inside the Wigwam: Chicago Presidential Conventions 1860–1996* (Chicago: Wild Onion Books, 1996), chapter 1; and Gordon Leidner, "How Lincoln Won the 1860 Republican Nomination," Great American History, http://www.greatamericanhistory.net/nomination.htm (accessed June 8, 2009).
9 William G. Mayer, "What the Founders Intended: Another Look at the Origins of the American Presidential Selection Process," in *The Making of the Presidential Candidates 2008*, ed. William G. Mayer (Lanham, MD: Rowman & Littlefield, 2008), 203–34.

10 Lawrence D. Longley and Neal R. Peirce, *The Electoral College Primer* (New Haven, CT: Yale University Press, 1996); and John P. Roche, "The Founding Fathers: A Reform Caucus in Action," *American Political Science Review* 55 (1961): 799–816.

11 Marty Cohen et al., *The Party Decides: Presidential Nominations Before and After Reform* (Chicago: University of Chicago Press, 2008), 50.

12 Robert E. DiClerico, "Evolution of the Presidential Nominating Process," in *Choosing Our Presidents: Debating the Presidential Nominating Process*, ed. Robert E. DiClerico and James W. Davis (Lanham, MD: Rowman & Littlefield, 2000), 3–26.

13 Austin Ranney, *Curing the Mischief of Faction: Party Reform in America* (Berkeley: University of California Press, 1975), 171–74.

14 Ranney, *Curing the Mischief of Faction*, 174–76; and DiClerico, "Evolution of the Presidential Nominating Process."

15 James W. Davis, *Presidential Primaries: Road to the White House* (New York: Thomas Y. Crowell, 1967), 24–26.

16 C. D. Allin, "The Presidential Primary," *Queen's Quarterly* 20 (1912): 92–99.

17 William Thomas Laprade, "The Nominating Primary," *North American Review* 20 (1914): 235–43.

18 Louise Overacker, *The Presidential Primary* (New York: Macmillan, 1926); and Richard L. Rubins, "Presidential Primaries: Continuities, Dimensions of Change, and Political Implications," in *The Party Symbol: Readings on Political Parties*, ed. William Crotty (San Francisco: W. H. Freeman, 1980), 126–47.

19 Percentages listed are from William H. Lucy, "Polls, Primaries, and Presidential Nominations," *Journal of Politics* 35 (1973): 830–48. For similar results see James R. Beniger, "Winning the Presidential Nomination: National Polls and State Primary Elections, 1936–1972," *Public Opinion Quarterly* 40 (1976): 22–38.

20 Theodore H. White, *The Making of the President 1960* (New York: Atheneum House, 1961); and Cohen et al., *The Party Decides*, 124–26.

21 William Carleton, "The Revolution in Presidential Nominating Conventions," *Political Science Quarterly* 72 (1957): 237.

22 *Mandate for Reform: A Report of the Commission on Party Structure and Delegate Selection to the Democratic National Committee* (Washington, DC: Democratic National Committee, 1970). Also, Theodore H. White, *The Making of the President 1964* (New York: Atheneum, 1965), 331–36; and Ranney, *Curing the Mischief of Faction*, 181–84.

23 Cohen et al., *The Party Decides*, 126–29; Theodore H. White, *The Making of the President 1968* (New York: Atheneum, 1969).

24 William Crotty and John S. Jackson III, *Presidential Primaries and Nominations* (Washington, DC: CQ Press, 1985), 29–31.

25 L. Sandy Maisel, *Parties and Elections in America: The Electoral Process* (New York: Random House, 1987), 171.

26 Lewis Chester, Godfrey Hodgson, and Bruce Page, *An American Melodrama: The Presidential Campaign of 1968* (New York: Viking Press, 1969), 153–54.

27 William J. Crotty, *Decision for the Democrats: Reforming the Party Structure* (Baltimore, MD: Johns Hopkins University Press, 1978), 59–103.

28 Austin Ranney, "Changing the Rules of the Nominating Game," in *Choosing the President*, ed. James David Barber (Englewood Cliffs, NJ: Prentice-Hall, 1974), 71–94.

29 William R. Keech and Donald R. Matthews, *The Party's Choice* (Washington, DC: Brookings Institution, 1976), 229–31; Gerald M. Pomper, "New Rules

and New Games in Presidential Nominations," *Journal of Politics* 41 (1979): 784–805; Howard L. Reiter, *Selecting the President: The Nominating Process in Transition* (Philadelphia: University of Pennsylvania Press, 1985).

30 The two Republican reform commissions were Delegate and Organization (DO) Commission (1969–1972) and Rule 29 Commission (1972–1974). For more information see Ranney, "Changing the Rules of the Nominating Game"; Richard A. Watson, *The Presidential Contest* (New York: Wiley, 1980); and William J. Crotty and Gary C. Jacobson, *American Parties in Decline* (Boston: Little, Brown, and Co., 1980).

31 William J. Crotty, *Political Reform and the American Experiment* (New York: Thomas Crowell, 1977), 267–95.

32 Thomas Holbrook, "Convention Bumps," comment posted August 12, 2008, http://election08data.blogspot.com/2008/08/convention-bumps.html (accessed July 12, 2009). Figure given is average post-convention bounce from 1964 to 2004.

2 Presidential Nomination Politics at the Dawn of the 21st Century

1 "How He Did It," *Newsweek*, November 17, 2008, 49.

2 William G. Mayer, "The Presidential Nominations," in *The Election of 2000*, ed. Gerald M. Pomper (New York: Chatham House, 2001), 12–45.

3 See for example Phillip Paolino and Daron R. Shaw, "Lifting the Hood on the Straight-Talk Express: Examining the McCain Phenomenon," *American Politics Research* 29 (2001): 483–506.

4 Wayne P. Steger, "Presidential Renomination Challenges in the 20th Century," *Presidential Studies Quarterly* 33 (2003): 827–52.

5 Mayer, "The Presidential Nominations," 29.

6 Mayer, "The Presidential Nominations."

7 Barry C. Burden, "The Nominations: Technology, Money, and Transferable Momentum," in *The Elections of 2004*, ed. Michael Nelson (Washington, DC: CQ Press, 2005), 18–41.

8 Burden, "The Nominations: Technology, Money, and Transferable Momentum."

9 Gerald M. Pomper, "The Nominating Contests and Conventions," in *The Election of 1976: Reports and Interpretations*, ed. Gerald Pomper (New York: David McKay, 1977), 1–34.

10 Steger, "Presidential Renomination Challenges in the 20th Century."

11 John A. Aldrich, *Before the Convention* (Chicago: University of Chicago Press, 1980).

12 Gerald M. Pomper, *Nominating the President: The Politics of Convention Choice* (Evanston, IL: Northwestern University Press, 1966).

13 Burden, "The Nominations: Technology, Money, and Transferable Momentum"; and Barry C. Burden, "United States Senators as Presidential Candidates," *Political Science Quarterly* 117 (2002): 81–102. For a more historical analysis dating back to the 1800s, see Aldrich, *Before the Convention*, 27–29.

14 Burden, "The Nominations: Technology, Money, and Transferable Momentum."

15 Other Republicans leaving the 2000 race early included former Tennessee senator Lamar Alexander, former vice president Dan Quayle, and political commentator Pat Buchanan who left to pursue the Reform Party's presidential nomination. Early 2008 withdrawals on the Republican side included Kansas senator Sam

Brownback, Jim Gilmore former Republican governor of Virginia, Tom Tancredo Republican member of the House of Representatives from Colorado, Tommy Thompson former Republican governor of Wisconsin, and on the Democratic side Thomas Vilsack former governor of Iowa.

16 Caroline Heldman, Susan J. Carroll, and Stephanie Olson, " 'She Brought Only a Skirt': Print Media Coverage of Elizabeth Dole's Bid for the Republican Presidential Nomination," *Political Communication* 22 (2005): 315–35; Sean Aday and James Devitt, "Style over Substance: Newspaper Coverage of Elizabeth Dole's Presidential Bid," *Harvard International Journal of Press/ Politics* 6 (2001): 52–73.

17 Kathleen A. Dolan, *Voting for Women: How the Public Evaluates Women Candidates* (Boulder, CO: Westview Press, 2004); Georgia Duerst-Lahti, "Presidential Elections: Gendered Space and the Case of 2004," in *Gender and Elections: Shaping the Future of American Politics*, ed. Susan J. Carroll and Richard L. Fox (New York: Cambridge University Press, 2006), 12–42.

18 Alice H. Eagly and Steven J. Karau, "Role Congruity Theory of Prejudice toward Female Leaders," *Psychological Review* 109 (2002): 573–98.

19 Arthur T. Hadley, *The Invisible Primary* (Englewood Cliffs, NJ: Prentice-Hall, 1976).

20 Mayer, "The Presidential Nominations," 30.

21 Accepting federal matching funds in 2008 were John Edwards, Christopher Dodd, Joe Biden, Dennis Kucinich, Tom Tancredo, and Duncan Hunter. Declining federal matching funds were Barack Obama, Hillary Clinton, John McCain, Mitt Romney, Rudy Giuliani, Mike Huckabee, Ron Paul, and Fred Thompson.

22 Robert G. Boatright, "Campaign Finance in the 2008 Election," in *The American Elections of 2008*, ed. Janet M. Box-Steffensmeier and Steven E. Schier (Lanham, MD: Rowman & Littlefield, 2009), 137–60.

23 See Wayne P. Steger, "How Did the Primary Vote Forecasts Fare in 2008?," *Presidential Studies Quarterly* 39 (2009): 141–54; Randall E. Adkins and Andrew J. Dowdle, "Overcoming Pitfalls in Forecasting Presidential Nominations," *Presidential Studies Quarterly* 35 (2005): 646–60; and William G. Mayer, "Forecasting Nominations," in *In Pursuit of the White House: How We Choose Our Presidential Nominees*, ed. William G. Mayer (Chatham, NJ: Chatham House, 1996), 44–71.

24 Marty Cohen et al., *The Party Decides: Presidential Nominations Before and After Reform* (Chicago: University of Chicago Press, 2008).

25 Cohen et al., *The Party Decides*, 11–12, 221–26.

26 Cohen et al., *The Party Decides*, 177, 338–44.

27 Cohen et al., *The Party Decides*, 345–48.

28 Gallup poll results were obtained from the Roper Center's iPoll, using the key words "Republican and nomination" or "Democratic and nomination" for the two years preceding each election.

29 For more about momentum see Aldrich, *Before the Convention*; Patrick J. Kenney and Tom W. Rice, "The Psychology of Political Momentum," *Political Research Quarterly* 47 (1994): 923–38; Thomas E. Patterson, *The Mass Media Election: How Americans Choose Their President* (New York: Praeger, 1980).

30 Iowa participation numbers from Barbara Norrander, "Democratic Marathon, Republican Sprint," in *The American Elections of 2008*, ed. Janet M. Box-Steffensmeier and Steven E. Schier (Lanham, MD: Rowman & Littlefield, 2009), 42–47. Iowa voting age population (VAP) from Michael McDonald,

United States Elections Project website, http://elections.gmu.edu/Turnout_2008G.html (accessed July 8, 2009).

31 Emmett H. Buell, Jr., " 'Locals' and 'Cosmopolitans': National, Regional, and State Newspaper Coverage of the New Hampshire Primary," in *Media and Momentum*, ed. Gary R. Orren and Nelson W. Polsby (Chatham, NJ: Chatham House, 1987), 60–103.

32 Barbara Norrander, "The Attrition Game: Initial Resources, Initial Contests and the Exit of Candidates During the US Presidential Primary Season," *British Journal of Political Science* 36 (2006): 487–507; Wayne P. Steger, Andrew J. Dowdle, and Randall E. Adkins, "The New Hampshire Effect in Presidential Nominations," *Political Research Quarterly* 57 (2004): 375–90.

33 In 2004, Howard Dean won his home-state primary in Vermont after he had withdrawn from the race.

34 Norrander, "Democratic Marathon, Republican Sprint," 49.

35 The 2008 Democratic race also included caucuses in American Samoa, Democrats Abroad, Virgin Islands, and Guam. Clinton won in American Samoa while Obama claimed victory in the other three. Texas held both a primary and a caucus, with Clinton winning the primary portion and Obama winning the caucus delegates.

36 Cohen et al., *The Party Decides*, 100.

37 John Parmelee, "Presidential Primary Videocassettes: How Candidates in the 2000 U.S. Presidential Primary Elections Framed Their Early Campaigns," *Political Communication* 19 (2002): 317–31; Clyde Wilcox, "Internet Fundraising in 2008: A New Model?," *The Forum*, Volume 6, Issue 1, Article 6 (2008), http://www.bepress.com/forum/vol6/iss1/art6 (accessed March 5, 2010).

38 Matthew Hindman, "The Real Lessons of Howard Dean: Reflections on the First Digital Campaign," *Perspectives on Politics* 3 (2005): 121–28; Jose Antonio Vargas, "Campaign.USA: With the Internet Comes a New Political 'Clickocracy'," *Washington Post*, April 1, 2008; Christine B. Williams and Girish "Jeff" Gulati, "What is a Social Network Worth?: Facebook and Vote Share in the 2008 Presidential Primaries" (paper presented at the annual meeting of the American Political Science Association convention, Boston, MA, August 28–31, 2008).

39 Jeffry Scott, "Countdown 2008: Road to the White House; McKinney gets Green Party Nomination for Presidency; Ex-House Rep from DeKalb on Most Ballots," *Atlanta Journal-Constitution*, July 13, 2008; Aaron Gould Sheinin, "Libertarians Pick Barr as Nominee," *Atlanta Journal-Constitution*, May 26, 2008.

40 *Guide to U.S. Elections*, 5th edition, volume 1 (Washington, DC: CQ Press, 2005), 190–91, 718, 730.

3 Is This a Fair Way to Select a Presidential Nominee?

1 Barbara Norrander, "Public Support for Presidential Nomination Reform," *Public Opinion Quarterly* 73 (2009): 578–89.

2 David S. Broder, "Endless Primaries Net Endless Candidacy," *Washington Post*, June 5, 1980; James L. Sundquist, "The Crisis of Competence in Our National Government," *Political Science Quarterly* 95 (1980): 183–208; James W. Ceaser, *Reforming the Reforms: A Critical Analysis of the Presidential Selection Process* (Cambridge, MA: Ballinger, 1982); and for a recap see James W. Davis, "The Case against the Current Primary-Centered System," in

Choosing Our Choices: Debating the Presidential Nominating Process, ed. Robert E. DiClerico and James W. Davis (Lanham, MD: Rowman & Littlefield, 2000), 27–30.

3 The averages are based on American National Election Studies surveys and collapse leaning independents with strong and weak partisans for both parties. These averages are based on votes for all major candidates and not just the two party candidates.

4 To calculate turnout in primaries, a state's potential electorate needs to be divided into the Democratic and Republican portions. These are citizens most likely to vote in each party's primaries or caucuses. While some states require voters to designate a party affiliation when they register to vote, about half the states do not do so. Thus, to figure out the partisan component of each state's electorate, another figure was needed that can be used across all states. One such figure would be the proportion of respondents who say they are Democrats or Republicans in their answers to the exit polls conducted at the time of each presidential election. Since one election exit poll may be swayed by the specific candidates running, an average over several years may be better. Thus, results from 1996 to 2004 exit polls were merged. Partisanship was measured based on the percent Democrat versus the percent Republicans. Independents are technically excluded from these percentages, but the effect is the same as distributing independents across the two parties in proportions that reflect the existing division between Democrats and Republicans. These resulting partisan proportions were multiplied by the number of potential voters in each state using a Census Bureau figure known as the voting age population. This is the number of state residents 18 or older. The final figure is the potential partisan electorate in each state. As an example, California has the largest voting age population in the nation in 2008 at 27,466,418 residents 18 or older. Californians are slightly more Democratic (54 percent) than Republican (46 percent). Thus the size of the potential Democratic electorate is 14,831,866 and the potential Republican electorate is 12,703,218.

5 Voting age population figures and 2008 general election turnout figure from Michael McDonald, United States Election Project, 2008 General Election Turnout Rates, http://elections.gmu.edu/Turnout_2008G.html (accessed July 8, 2009).

6 Louise Overacker, *The Presidential Primary* (New York: Macmillan, 1926), 244–51.

7 Jack Moran and Mark Fenster, "Voter Turnout in Presidential Primaries: A Diachronic Analysis," *American Politics Quarterly* 10 (1982): 453–76; Overacker, *The Presidential Primary*; Austin Ranney, *Participation in American Presidential Nominations, 1976* (Washington, DC: American Enterprise Institute, 1977); Lawrence S. Rothenberg and Richard A. Brody, "Participation in Presidential Primaries," *Western Political Quarterly* 41 (1988): 253–71.

8 John G. Geer, "Assessing the Representativeness of Electorates in Presidential Primaries," *American Journal of Political Science* 32 (1988): 929–45; Karen M. Kaufman, James G. Gimpel, and Adam H. Hoffman, "A Promise Fulfilled?: Open Primaries and Representation," *Journal of Politics* 65 (2003): 457–76; Barbara Norrander, "Ideological Representativeness of Presidential Primary Voters," *American Journal of Political Science* 33 (1989): 570–87. For a review of other findings see Barbara Norrander, "Field Essay: Presidential Nomination Politics in the Post-Reform Era," *Political Research Quarterly* 49 (1996): 887–89.

9 Marty Cohen et al., *The Party Decides: Presidential Nominations Before and After Reform* (Chicago: University of Chicago Press, 2008); David S. Broder, "No Way to Choose a President," *Washington Post*, December 31, 2003.

10 Nelson W. Polsby, *Consequences of Party Reform* (New York: Oxford University Press, 1983).

11 Frank Newport, "Obama Gains among Former Clinton Supporters," *Gallup Poll*, September 2, 2008.

12 Walter J. Stone, Lonna Rae Atkeson, and Ronald B. Rapoport, "Turning On or Turning Off?: Mobilization and Demobilization Effects of Participation in Presidential Nomination Campaigns," *American Journal of Political Science* 36 (1992): 665–91.

13 Barbara Norrander, "Explaining Cross-State Variation in Independents," *American Journal of Political Science* 33 (1989): 516–36.

14 *Democratic Party v. Wisconsin ex rel. La Follette*, 450 U.S. 107 (1981); *Tashjian v. Republican Party of Connecticut*, 479 U.S. 208 (1986); *California Democratic Party v. Jones*, 530 U.S. 567 (2000).

15 Emmett H. Buell, Jr., "The Rise of a Primary-Dominated Process," in *Enduring Controversies in Presidential Nominating Politics*, ed. Emmett H. Buell, Jr. and William G. Mayer (Pittsburgh: University of Pittsburgh Press, 2004), 193–219.

16 The New Hampshire registration figures are from June 13, 2008, Secretary of State, Election Division, http://www.sos.nh.gov/Voters%20on%20the%20 Checklist%20by%20Party%202008-06-12.pdf (accessed March 5, 2010). The partisanship of voters in 2008 New Hampshire primaries are from the media exit polls.

17 William G. Mayer, "Caucuses: How They Work, What Difference They Make," in *In Pursuit of the White House: How We Choose Our Presidential Nominees*, ed. William G. Mayer (Chatham, NJ: Chatham House, 1996), 105–57.

18 Mayer, "Caucuses: How They Work, What Difference They Make," 129.

19 Mayer, "Caucuses: How They Work, What Difference They Make," 105–57; Barbara Norrander, "Nomination Choices: Caucus and Primary Outcomes, 1976–1988," *American Journal of Political Science* 37 (1993): 343–64.

20 Walter J. Stone, Ronald B. Rapoport, and Alan I. Abramowitz, "Candidate Support in Presidential Nomination Campaigns: The Case of Iowa in 1984," *Journal of Politics* 54 (1992): 1074–97.

21 Byron Shafer and Amber Wichowsky, "Institutional Structure and Democratic Values: A Research Note on a Natural Experiment," *The Forum*, Volume 7, Issue 2, Article 2 (2009), http://www.bepress.com/forum/vol7/iss2/art2 (accessed March 5, 2010).

22 *Guide to U.S. Elections*, 5th edition, volume 1 (Washington, DC: CQ Press, 2005), 432–33.

23 Republican National Committee, *Call for the 2008 Republican National Convention*, November 9, 2007.

24 Democratic National Committee, *Call for the 2008 Democratic National Convention*, February 2, 2007.

25 This analysis uses the same partisan divisions of the voting age population as was employed in the calculation of primary turnout. For this part of the analysis, only pledged delegates are included and these are the original delegate totals given to a state before bonuses or punishments.

26 Randall E. Adkins and Kent A. Kirwan, "What Role Does the 'Federalism Bonus' Play in Presidential Selection?," *Publius: The Journal of Federalism* 32 (2002): 71–90.

27 The Democratic analysis excluded Texas, which held both a primary and a caucus. The Republican analysis excluded Washington state and West Virginia, which also held both a primary and a caucus or convention.

28 Adkins and Kirwan, "What Role Does the 'Federalism Bonus' Play in Presidential Selection?," 81.

29 The Republican Party in 2000 also tried a bonus delegate system to encourage states to hold later primaries. This incentive did not work. Few states were willing to hold later primaries to receive additional delegates. Thus, the Republican Party dropped the bonus system for the 2004 primaries. Instead, the Republican Party in 2004 began to add their own version of superdelegates with automatic seats for Republican National Committee members.

30 Howard L. Reiter, *Selecting the President: The Nominating Process in Transition* (Philadelphia: University of Pennsylvania Press, 1985), 66.

31 William G. Mayer, "Superdelegates: Reforming the Reforms Revisited," in *Reforming the Presidential Nomination Process*, ed. Steven S. Smith and Melanie J. Springer (Washington, DC: Brookings Institution, 2009), 85–108.

32 Priscilla L. Southwell, "The 1984 Democratic Nomination Process: The Significance of Unpledged Superdelegates," *American Politics Quarterly* 14 (1986): 75–88.

33 Jesse Jackson attempted in 1988 to again get the number of superdelegates reduced, but the Democratic National Committee restored all its members as delegates for the 1992 convention. Mayer, "Superdelegates: Reforming the Reforms Revisited."

34 Shailagh Murray and Paul Kane, "In Background, a Battle for Superdelegates: Clinton Ahead Among Party Leaders, but Threat of a Wholesale Shift Remains," *Washington Post*, January 30, 2008; Marcella Bombardieri, "Superdelegates Could Prove Kingmakers; Candidates Court those Not Obliged to do Voters' Will," *Boston Globe*, February 1, 2008.

35 Mayer, "Superdelegates: Reforming the Reforms Revisited." The Republican Party did have a ban on ex officio delegates between 1976 and 2000, but this did not change the proportions of Republican governors, senators, or House members who have been convention delegates.

36 Cohen et al., *The Party Decides*.

37 Each state receives an additional 15 percent of delegates for pledged party and elected officials. The support for these pledged PEOs is distributed by the statewide vote. Including the pledged PEOs in the totals results in two-thirds of a state's pledged delegates being allocated on the basis of district votes and one-third on the results at the state level.

38 See Brian Arbour, "Even Closer, Even Longer: What If the 2008 Democratic Party Used Republican Rules?," *The Forum*, Volume 7, Issue 2, Article 3 (2009), http://www.bepress.com/forum/vol7/iss2/art3 (accessed March 5, 2010).

39 Delegate projections are based on primary votes and caucuses which reported support levels for the candidates.

40 James I. Lengle and Byron Shafer, "Primary Rules, Political Power, and Social Change," *American Political Science Review* 70 (1976): 25–40. Slightly different results were found by Thomas H. Hammond, "Another Look at the Role of 'The Rules' in the 1972 Democratic Presidential Primaries," *Western Political Quarterly* 33 (1980): 50–72. No biases were found by Gerald M. Pomper, "New Rules and New Games in Presidential Nominations," *Journal of Politics* 41 (1979): 784–805.

41 See Arbour, "Even Closer, Even Longer."

42 Emmett H. Buell, Jr., "The Changing Face of the New Hampshire Primary," in *In Pursuit of the White House 2000*, ed. William G. Mayer (Chatham, NJ: Chatham House, 2000), 87–144.

43 Peverill Squire, "Iowa and the Nomination Process," in *The Iowa Caucuses and the Presidential Nominating Process*, ed. Peverill Squire (Boulder, CO: Westview Press, 1989), 1–19.

44 Cullen Murphy, "Primary Considerations," *Atlantic Monthly*, April 2004, 148–49.

45 Michael S. Lewis-Beck and Peverill Squire, "Iowa: The Most Representative State?," *PS: Political Science & Politics* 42 (2009): 39–44.

46 Quoted in Ewen MacAskill, "Presidential Race 2008: Slow Road from Iowa to Washington to be Replaced by Fast-Track Selection: Super Duper Tuesday Could Shorten Race to Win the Presidential Nomination," *Guardian* (London), April 5, 2007, 29.

47 Lonna Rae Atkeson and Cherie D. Maestas, "Meaningful Participation and the Evolution of the Reformed Presidential Nominating System," *PS: Political Science & Politics* 42 (2009): 59–64; William G. Mayer and Andrew E. Busch, *The Front-Loading Problem in Presidential Nominations* (Washington, DC: Brooking Institution, 2004).

48 Michael J. Robinson and Margaret A. Sheehan, *Over the Wire and on TV* (New York: Russell Sage Foundation, 1983); and Henry E. Brady and Richard Johnston, "What's the Primary Message: Horse Race or Issue Journalism?," in *Media and Momentum*, ed. Gary R. Orren and Nelson W. Polsby (Chatham, NJ: Chatham House, 1987), 127–86.

4 Alternative Methods for Nominating Presidents

1 National Association of Secretaries of State, *The Case for Regional Presidential Primaries in 2012 and Beyond*, February 2008, http://nass.org/index.php?option=com_content&task=view&id=74&Itemid=210 (accessed November 19, 2009).

2 Larry J. Sabato, "Picking Presidential Nominees: Time for a New Regime," in *Reforming the Presidential Nomination Process*, ed. Steven S. Smith and Melanie J. Springer (Washington, DC: Brookings Institution, 2009), 136–50.

3 Kevin J. Coleman, *Presidential Nominating Process: Current Issues*, CRS Report for Congress, RL34222, April 11, 2008, http://fpc.state.gov/documents/organization/106173.pdf (accessed March 5, 2010).

4 Barbara Norrander, *Super Tuesday: Regional Politics and Presidential Primaries* (Lexington: University Press of Kentucky, 1992); and Barbara Norrander, "Lessons from the 1988 Southern Regional Primary," in *The Rise of the West in Presidential Elections* (Salt Lake City: University of Utah Press, forthcoming).

5 Barbara Norrander, "Public Support for Presidential Nomination Reform," *Public Opinion Quarterly* 73 (2009): 578–89.

6 Dan Balz, "Schwarzenegger Aims to Lift California's Clout; State Seeks Influence Befitting Its Size in '08 Race and Beyond," *Washington Post*, March 27, 2007.

7 Republican National Committee, *Nominating Future Presidents* (Washington, DC: Republican National Committee, 2000); FairVote, "The Delaware Plan," http://www.fairvote.org/?page=2064 (accessed November 20, 2009).

8 *Guide to U.S. Elections*, 5th edition, volume 1 (Washington, DC: CQ Press, 2005), 322–23.

9 William G. Mayer and Andrew E. Busch, *The Front-Loading Problem in Presidential Nominations* (Washington, DC: Brookings Institution, 2004), 105–09.

10 Greg Giroux, " 'Front-loading' Frustration Spurs GOP Talk of a Fix," CQ Today Online News, January 20, 2008, http://www.cqpolitics.com/wmspage.cfm?parm1=5&docID=news-000002658056 (accessed January 22, 2008).

11 Robert D. Loevy, *The Flawed Path to the Presidency, 1992: Unfairness and Inequality in the Presidential Selection Process* (Albany: State University of

New York Press, 1995); and Robert D. Loevy, *The Manipulated Path to the White House, 1996: Maximizing Advantage in the Presidential Selection Process* (Lanham, MD: University Press of America, 1998).

12 Giroux, " 'Front-loading' Frustration Spurs GOP Talk of a Fix"; and Elaine C. Kamarck, *Primary Politics: How Presidential Candidates Have Shaped the Modern Nominating System* (Washington, DC: Brookings Institution Press, 2009), 175–85.

13 Thomas Gangale, *From the Primaries to the Polls* (Westport, CT: Praeger, 2008).

14 The region and subregion groups are from the Fair and Representative Presidential Primaries Act of 2009, S. 1433.

15 Bruce E. Altschuler, "Selecting Presidential Nominees by National Primary: An Idea Whose Time Has Come?," *The Forum*, Volume 5, Issue 4, Article 5 (2008), http://www.bepress.com/forum/vol5/iss4/art5 (accessed March 5, 2010).

16 Woodrow Wilson, First Annual Message to Congress, December 2, 1913, available at the Miller Center of Public Affairs, University of Virginia, http://millercenter.org/scripps/archive/speeches/detail/3789 (accessed November 23, 2009).

17 Altschuler, "Selecting Presidential Nominees by National Primary."

18 P. Orman Ray, "Reform of Presidential Nominating Methods," *Annals of the American Academy of Political and Social Science* 106 (1923): 63–71.

19 For arguments for and against the national primary see Altschuler, "Selecting Presidential Nominees by National Primary."

20 Sharon Begley, "When Math Warps Elections," *Newsweek*, February 4, 2008, 18.

21 Mayer and Busch, *The Front-Loading Problem in Presidential Nominations*, 96.

22 Information on current runoff elections is found in Charles S. Bullock III, Ronald Keith Gaddie, and Anders Ferrington, "System Structure, Campaign Stimuli, and Voter Falloff in Runoff Primaries," *Journal of Politics* 64 (2002): 1210–24.

23 Steven J. Brams and Peter C. Fishburn, "Approval Voting," *American Political Science Review* 72 (1978): 831–47; and Steven J. Brams and Dudley R. Herschbach, "The Science of Elections," *Science* 292 (May 25, 2001): 1449.

24 FairVote, "How Instant Runoff Voting Compares to Alternative Reforms," http://www.fairvote.org/how-instant-runoff-voting-compares-to-alternative-reforms/ (accessed March 8, 2010).

25 Fair Vote, "Delegating Democracy: How the Parties Can Make their Presidential Nominating Contests More Democratic," http://www.fairvote.org/fixtheprimaries/media/Delegating%20Democracy.pdf (accessed November 25, 2009).

26 Bob Von Sternberg and Steve Brandt, "Ballot Count By Hand Starts in Minneapolis," *Star Tribune*, November 4, 2009.

27 John Haskell, *Fundamentally Flawed: Understanding and Reforming Presidential Primaries* (Lanham, MD: Rowman & Littlefield, 1996). For basic discussions of voting rules and selection criteria see Kenneth Arrow, *Social Choice and Individual Values*, 2nd edition (New Haven, CT: Yale University Press, 1963) and William H. Riker, *Liberalism Against Populism* (San Francisco: W. H. Freeman, 1982).

28 Thomas Cronin and Robert Loevy, "The Case for a National Pre-Primary Convention Plan," *Public Opinion* 5 (1983): 50–53; Haskell, *Fundamentally Flawed*, 74–76.

29 Mayer and Busch, *The Front-Loading Problem in Presidential Nominations*, 109–14.

30 William G. Mayer and Andrew E. Busch, "Can the Federal Government Reform the Presidential Nomination Process?," *Election Law Journal* 3 (2004): 613–25; Richard L. Hasen, "'Too Plain for Argument?': The Uncertain Congressional Power to Require Parties to Choose Presidential Nominees through Direct and Equal Primaries," *Northwestern University Law Review* 102 (2008): 2009–2019; and testimonies of William Mayer and Richard Hasen before the United States Senate, Committee on Rules and Administration, September 19, 2007 on S. 1905, Presidential Primary and Caucus Act of 2007.

31 *Cousins v. Wigoda*, 419 U.S. 477 (1974); *Democratic Party v. Wisconsin ex rel. La Follette*, 450 U.S. 107 (1981); *Tashjian v. Republican Party of Connecticut*, 479 U.S. 208 (1986); *California Democratic Party v. Jones*, 530 U.S. 567 (2000).

32 Quoted in Giroux, "'Front-loading' Frustration Spurs GOP Talk of a Fix."

33 Frank Leone, "DNC Change Commission Adopts Report," DemRulz, comment posted on December 30, 2009, http://demrulz.org/?p=1239 (accessed December 31, 2009); "The Rules of the Republican Party," as adopted by the 2008 Republican National Convention, September 1, 2008; *Report of the Democratic Change Commission* (Washington, DC: Democratic National Committee, 2009), http://my.democrats.org/page/content/changecommissionreport (accessed March 8, 2010).

34 "House Votes to Eliminate Presidential Primary," Associated Press State & Local Wire, April 8, 2003.

35 Michael J. Malbin, "Small Donors, Large Donors and the Internet: The Case for Public Financing after Obama," The Campaign Finance Institute, April 2009, http://www.cfinst.org/pr/prRelease.aspx?ReleaseID=228 (accessed December 9, 2009).

36 Malbin, "Small Donors, Large Donors and the Internet."

37 *Buckley v. Valeo*, 424 U.S. 1 (1976).

38 Malbin, "Small Donors, Large Donors and the Internet."

39 *Davis v. Federal Election Commission*, 501 F. Supp. 2d 22 (2008).

5 Oddities, Biases, and Strengths of U.S. Presidential Nomination Politics

1 *Guide to U.S. Elections*, 5th edition, volume 1 (Washington, DC: CQ Press, 2005), 463–81.

2 Marty Cohen et al., *The Party Decides: Presidential Nominations Before and After Reform* (Chicago: University of Chicago Press, 2008), 112–18.

3 Rhodes Cook, *The Presidential Nominating Process* (Lanham, MD: Rowman & Littlefield, 2004), chapter 5; James A. McCann, "The Emerging International Trend toward Open Presidential Primaries: The American Presidential Nomination Process in Comparative Perspective," in *The Making of the Presidential Candidates 2004*, ed. William G. Mayer (Lanham, MD: Rowman & Littlefield, 2004), 265–93.

4 Anthony Corrado, "Financing the 1996 Election," in *The Election of 1996*, ed. Gerald M. Pomper (Chatham, NJ: Chatham House, 1997), 135–72.

5 Maurcie Duverger, *Political Parties: Their Organization and Activity in the Modern State*, translated by Barbara North and Robert North (New York: Wiley, 1954).

6 Michael G. Hagen, "Press Treatment of Front-Runners," in *In the Pursuit of the White House*, ed. William G. Mayer (Chatham, NJ: Chatham House, 1996), 190–219.

7 Phillip Paolino and Daron R. Shaw, "Lifting the Hood on the Straight-Talk Express: Examining the McCain Phenomenon," *American Politics Research* 29 (2001): 483–506.

8 The 2008 media coverage as analyzed by the Project for Excellence in Journalism and the Joan Shorenstein Center on Press, Politics and Public Policy at Harvard University. "The Invisible Primary—Invisible No Longer," http://www.journalism.org/node/8187; "McCain Wins the Coverage Battle as Media Move to Anoint Him," http://www.journalism.org/node/9610; "Post-Pennsylvania Spin Drowns Out McCain," http://www.journalism.org/node/10824 (accessed December 17, 2009).

9 David C. Barker and Adam B. Lawrence, "Media Favoritism and Presidential Nominations: Reviving the Direct Effects Model," *Political Communications* 23 (2006): 41–59; David A. Jones, "Political Talk Radio: The Limbaugh Effect on Primary Voters," *Political Communication* 15 (1998): 367–81.

10 Wayne Steger, Andrew Dowdle, and Randall Adkins, "Seeking Competitive Advantage: How Presidential Candidates and Party Networks Adapt to Times of Social, Economic, and Technological Change" (paper presented at the State of the Parties Conference, Ray Bliss Institute, University of Akron, October 15–16, 2009).

11 V. O. Key, *Politics, Parties, and Pressure Groups*, 3rd edition (New York: Thomas Y. Crowell, 1952), 329; Frank J. Sorauf, *Party Politics in America*, 3rd edition (Boston: Little, Brown, 1976).

12 Seth E. Masket, Michael T. Heaney, Joanne M. Miller, and Dara Z. Strolovitch, "Networking the Parties: A Comparative Study of Democratic and Republican National Convention Delegates in 2008" (paper presented at the annual meeting of the American Political Science Association, Toronto, Ontario, Canada, September 3–6, 2009).

13 James Q. Wilson, *The Amateur Democrat: Club Politics in Three Cities* (Chicago: University of Chicago Press, 1962).

14 Jonathan Alter, "Poof Goes the Purple Dream," *Newsweek*, February 23, 2009, 33.

15 George F. Will, "Messy, But Not a Mess," *Newsweek*, November 5, 2007, 72.

Bibliography

Aday, Sean, and James Devitt. "Style over Substance: Newspaper Coverage of Elizabeth Dole's Presidential Bid." *Harvard International Journal of Press/Politics* 6 (2001): 52–73.

Adkins, Randall E., and Andrew J. Dowdle. "Overcoming Pitfalls in Forecasting Presidential Nominations." *Presidential Studies Quarterly* 35 (2005): 646–60.

Adkins, Randall E., and Kent A. Kirwan. "What Role Does the 'Federalism Bonus' Play in Presidential Selection?" *Publius: The Journal of Federalism* 32 (2002): 71–90.

Aldrich, John A. *Before the Convention*. Chicago: University of Chicago Press, 1980.

Allin, C. D. "The Presidential Primary." *Queen's Quarterly* 20 (1912): 92–99.

Alter, Jonathan. "Poof Goes the Purple Dream." *Newsweek*, February 23, 2009.

Altschuler, Bruce E. "Selecting Presidential Nominees by National Primary: An Idea Whose Time Has Come?" *The Forum*, Volume 5, Issue 4, Article 5 (2008), http://www.bepress.com/forum/vol5/iss4/art5 (accessed March 5, 2010).

Arbour, Brian. "Even Closer, Even Longer: What If the 2008 Democratic Party Used Republican Rules?" *The Forum*, Volume 7, Issue 2, Article 3 (2009), http://www.bepress.com/forum/vol7/iss2/art3 (accessed March 5, 2010).

Arrow, Kenneth. *Social Choice and Individual Values*, 2nd edition. New Haven, CT: Yale University Press, 1963.

Atkeson, Lonna Rae, and Cherie D. Maestas. "Meaningful Participation and the Evolution of the Reformed Presidential Nominating System." *PS: Political Science & Politics* 42 (2009): 59–64.

"Back from the Dead." *Newsweek*, November 17, 2008.

Balz, Dan. "Schwarzenegger Aims to Lift California's Clout; State Seeks Influence Befitting Its Size in '08 Race and Beyond." *Washington Post*, March 27, 2007.

Barker, David C., and Adam B. Lawrence. "Media Favoritism and Presidential Nominations: Reviving the Direct Effects Model." *Political Communications* 23 (2006): 41–59.

Begley, Sharon. "When Math Warps Elections." *Newsweek*, February 4, 2008.

Beniger, James R. "Winning the Presidential Nomination: National Polls and State Primary Elections, 1936–1972." *Public Opinion Quarterly* 40 (1976): 22–38.

Boatright, Robert G. "Campaign Finance in the 2008 Election." In *The American Elections of 2008*, edited by Janet M. Box-Steffensmeier and Steven E. Schier, 137–60. Lanham, MD: Rowman & Littlefield, 2009.

Bombardieri, Marcella. "Superdelegates Could Prove Kingmakers; Candidates Court those Not Obliged to do Voters' Will." *Boston Globe*, February 1, 2008.

Brady, Henry E., and Richard Johnston. "What's the Primary Message: Horse Race or Issue Journalism?" In *Media and Momentum*, edited by Gary R. Orren and Nelson W. Polsby, 127–86. Chatham, NJ: Chatham House, 1987.

Brams, Steven J., and Peter C. Fishburn. "Approval Voting." *American Political Science Review* 72 (1978): 831–47.

Brams, Steven J., and Dudley R. Herschbach. "The Science of Elections." *Science* 292 (2001): 1449.

Broder, David S. "Endless Primaries Net Endless Candidacy." *Washington Post*, June 5, 1980.

———. "No Way to Choose a President." *Washington Post*, December 31, 2003.

Buell, Emmett H., Jr. "'Locals' and 'Cosmopolitans': National, Regional, and State Newspaper Coverage of the New Hampshire Primary." In *Media and Momentum*, edited by Gary R. Orren and Nelson W. Polsby, 60–103. Chatham, NJ: Chatham House, 1987.

———. "The Changing Face of the New Hampshire Primary." In *In Pursuit of the White House 2000*, edited by William G. Mayer, 87–144. Chatham, NJ: Chatham House, 2000.

———. "The Rise of a Primary-Dominated Process." In *Enduring Controversies in Presidential Nominating Politics*, edited by Emmett H. Buell, Jr. and William G. Mayer, 193–219. Pittsburgh: University of Pittsburgh Press, 2004.

Bullock, Charles S., III, Ronald Keith Gaddie, and Anders Ferrington. "System Structure, Campaign Stimuli, and Voter Falloff in Runoff Primaries." *Journal of Politics* 64 (2002): 1210–24.

Burden, Barry C. "United States Senators as Presidential Candidates." *Political Science Quarterly* 117 (2002): 81–102.

———. "The Nominations: Technology, Money, and Transferable Momentum." In *The Elections of 2004*, edited by Michael Nelson, 18–41. Washington, DC: CQ Press, 2005.

Carleton, William. "The Revolution in the Presidential Nominating Conventions." *Political Science Quarterly* 72 (1957): 224–40.

Ceaser, James W. *Reforming the Reforms: A Critical Analysis of the Presidential Selection Process.* Cambridge, MA: Ballinger, 1982.

"Chaotic Primary System Needs Reform." *Kansas City Star*, February 7, 2008.

Chester, Lewis, Godfrey Hodgson, and Bruce Page. *An American Melodrama: The Presidential Campaign of 1968.* New York: Viking Press, 1969.

Cohen, Marty, David Karol, Hans Noel, and John Zaller. *The Party Decides: Presidential Nominations Before and After Reform.* Chicago: University of Chicago Press, 2008.

Coleman, Kevin J. *Presidential Nominating Process: Current Issues.* CRS Report for Congress, RL34222, April 11, 2008. Available at http://fpc.state.gov/documents/organization/106173.pdf (accessed March 5, 2010).

Cook, Rhodes. "2000 Primary and Caucuses: Who Can Vote and How They Voted." Available at http://www.rhodescook.com/analysis/presidential_primaries/national/natchart.html (accessed July 13, 2009).

———. "2004: The Voting Begins." Available at http://www.rhodescook.com/primary.analysis.html (accessed July 13, 2009).

———. *The Presidential Nominating Process*. Lanham, MD: Rowman & Littlefield, 2004.

———. *Race for the Presidency: Winning the 2008 Nomination*. Washington, DC: CQ Press, 2008.

Corrado, Anthony. "Financing the 1996 Election." In *The Election of 1996*, edited by Gerald M. Pomper, 135–72. Chatham, NJ: Chatham House, 1997.

Cronin, Thomas, and Robert Loevy. "The Case for a National Pre-Primary Convention Plan." *Public Opinion* 5 (1983): 50–53.

Crotty, William J. *Political Reform and the American Experiment*. New York: Thomas Crowell, 1977.

———. *Decision for the Democrats: Reforming the Party Structure*. Baltimore, MD: Johns Hopkins University Press, 1978.

Crotty, William, and John S. Jackson III. *Presidential Primaries and Nominations*. Washington, DC: CQ Press, 1985.

Crotty, William J., and Gary C. Jacobson. *American Parties in Decline*. Boston: Little, Brown, and Co., 1980.

Davis, James W. *Presidential Primaries: Road to the White House*. New York: Thomas Y. Crowell, 1967.

———. "The Case against the Current Primary-Centered System." In *Choosing Our Choices: Debating the Presidential Nominating Process*, edited by Robert E. DiClerico and James W. Davis, 27–30. Lanham, MD: Rowman & Littlefield, 2000.

Democratic National Committee. *Mandate for Reform: A Report of the Commission on Party Structure and Delegate Selection to the Democratic National Committee*. Washington, DC: Democratic National Committee, 1970.

———. *Call for the 2008 Democratic National Convention*. Washington, DC: Democratic National Committee, 2007.

———. *Report of the Democratic Change Commission*, Washington, DC: Democratic National Committee, 2009. Available at http://my.democrats.org/page/content/changecommissionreport (accessed March 8, 2010).

"Democrats' Chaotic Caucus Begs for Regional Reform." *Santa Fe New Mexican*, February 7, 2008.

DiClerico, Robert E. "Evolution of the Presidential Nominating Process." In *Choosing Our Choices: Debating the Presidential Nominating Process*, edited by Robert E. DiClerico and James W. Davis, 3–26. Lanham, MD: Rowman & Littlefield, 2000.

Dolan, Kathleen A. *Voting for Women: How the Public Evaluates Women Candidates*. Boulder, CO: Westview Press, 2004.

Duerst-Lahti, Georgia. "Presidential Elections: Gendered Space and the Case of 2004." In *Gender and Elections: Shaping the Future of American Politics*, edited by Susan J. Carroll and Richard L. Fox, 12–42. New York: Cambridge University Press, 2006.

Duverger, Maurice. *Political Parties: Their Organization and Activity in the Modern State*, translated by Barbara North and Robert North. New York: Wiley, 1954.

Eagly, Alice H., and Steven J. Karau. "Role Congruity Theory of Prejudice toward Female Leaders." *Psychological Review* 109 (2002): 573–98.

FairVote. "The Delaware Plan." Available at http://www.fairvote.org/?page=2064 (accessed November 20, 2009).

————. "Delegating Democracy: How the Parties Can Make their Presidential Nominating Contests More Democratic." Available at http://www.fairvote.org/fixtheprimaries/media/Delegating%20Democracy.pdf(accessed November 25, 2009).

————. "How Instant Runoff Voting Compares to Alternative Reforms." Available at http://www.fairvote.org/how-instant-runoff-voting-compares-to-alternative-reforms/ (accessed March 8, 2010).

Gangale, Thomas. *From the Primaries to the Polls*. Westport, CT: Praeger, 2008.

Geer, John G. "Assessing the Representativeness of Electorates in Presidential Primaries." *American Journal of Political Science* 32 (1988): 929–45.

Giroux, Greg. "'Front-loading' Frustration Spurs GOP Talk of a Fix." CQ Today Online News, January 20, 2008. Available at http://www.cqpolitics.com/wmspage.cfm?parm1=5&docID=news-000002658056 (accessed January 22, 2008).

Guide to U.S. Elections, 5th edition, volume 1. Washington, DC: CQ Press, 2005.

Hadley, Arthur T. *The Invisible Primary*. Englewood Cliffs, NJ: Prentice-Hall, 1976.

Hagen, Michael G. "Press Treatment of Front-Runners." In *In the Pursuit of the White House*, edited by William G. Mayer, 190–219. Chatham, NJ: Chatham House, 1996.

Hammond, Thomas H. "Another Look at the Role of 'The Rules' in the 1972 Democratic Presidential Primaries." *Western Political Quarterly* 33 (1980): 50–72.

Hasen, Richard L. "'Too Plain for Argument?': The Uncertain Congressional Power to Require Parties to Choose Presidential Nominees through Direct and Equal Primaries." *Northwestern University Law Review* 102 (2008): 2009–2019.

Haskell, John. *Fundamentally Flawed: Understanding and Reforming Presidential Primaries*. Lanham, MD: Rowman & Littlefield, 1996.

Heldman, Caroline, Susan J. Carroll, and Stephanie Olson. "'She Brought Only a Skirt': Print Media Coverage of Elizabeth Dole's Bid for the Republican Presidential Nomination." *Political Communication* 22 (2005): 315–35.

"A Helter-Skelter Primary System." *The Oregonian*, January 2, 2008.

Hindman, Matthew. "The Real Lessons of Howard Dean: Reflections on the First Digital Campaign." *Perspectives on Politics* 3 (2005): 121–28.

Holbrook, Thomas. "Convention Bumps." Posted August 12, 2008. Available at http://election08data.blogspot.com/2008/08/convention-bumps.html (accessed July 12, 2009).

"House Votes to Eliminate Presidential Primary." Associated Press State & Local Wire, April 8, 2003.

"How He Did It." *Newsweek*, November 17, 2008.

Jones, David A. "Political Talk Radio: The Limbaugh Effect on Primary Voters." *Political Communication* 15 (1998): 367–81.

Kamarck, Elaine C. *Primary Politics: How Presidential Candidates Have Shaped the Modern Nominating System*. Washington, DC: Brookings Institution Press, 2009.

Kaufman, Karen M., James G. Gimpel, and Adam H. Hoffman. "A Promise Fulfilled?: Open Primaries and Representation." *Journal of Politics* 65 (2003): 457–76.

Keech, William R., and Donald R. Matthews. *The Party's Choice*. Washington, DC: Brookings Institution, 1976.

Kenney, Patrick J., and Tom W. Rice. "The Psychology of Political Momentum." *Political Research Quarterly* 47 (1994): 923–38.

Key, V. O. *Politics, Parties, and Pressure Groups*, 3rd edition. New York: Thomas Y. Crowell, 1952.

Laprade, William Thomas. "The Nominating Primary." *North American Review* 20 (1914): 235–43.

Leidner, Gordon. "How Lincoln Won the 1860 Republican Nomination." Great American History. Available at http://www.greatamericanhistory.net/nomination.htm (accessed June 8, 2009).

Lengle, James I., and Byron Shafer. "Primary Rules, Political Power, and Social Change." *American Political Science Review* 70 (1976): 25–40.

Leone, Frank. "DNC Change Commission Adopts Report." DemRulz, comment posted on December 30, 2009, http://demrulz.org/?p=1239 (accessed December 31, 2009).

"Let it Start Now." *New York Times*, January 4, 2008.

"Let's Switch to Regional Primaries." *Columbus Dispatch*, January 6, 2008.

Lewis-Beck, Michael S., and Peverill Squire. "Iowa: The Most Representative State?" *PS: Political Science & Politics* 42 (2009): 39–44.

Loevy, Robert D. *The Flawed Path to the Presidency, 1992: Unfairness and Inequality in the Presidential Selection Process*. Albany: State University of New York Press, 1995.

———. *The Manipulated Path to the White House, 1996: Maximizing Advantage in the Presidential Selection Process*. Lanham, MD: University Press of America, 1998.

Longley, Lawrence D., and Neal R. Peirce. *The Electoral College Primer*. New Haven, CT: Yale University Press, 1996.

Lucy, William H. "Polls, Primaries, and Presidential Nominations." *Journal of Politics* 35 (1973): 830–48.

MacAskill, Ewen. "Presidential Race 2008: Slow Road from Iowa to Washington to be Replaced by Fast-Track Selection: Super Duper Tuesday Could Shorten Race to Win the Presidential Nomination." *Guardian* (London), April 5, 2007.

Maisel, L. Sandy. *Parties and Elections in America: The Electoral Process*. New York: Random House, 1987.

Malbin, Michael J. "Small Donors, Large Donors and the Internet: The Case for Public Financing after Obama." The Campaign Finance Institute, April 2009. Available at http://www.cfinst.org/pr/prRelease.aspx?ReleaseID=228 (accessed December 9, 2009).

Masket, Seth E., Michael T. Heaney, Joanne M. Miller, and Dara Z. Strolovitch. "Networking the Parties: A Comparative Study of Democratic and Republican National Convention Delegates in 2008." Paper presented at the annual meeting of the American Political Science Association, Toronto, Ontario, Canada, September 3–6, 2009.

Mayer, William G. "Caucuses: How They Work, What Difference They Make." In *In Pursuit of the White House: How We Choose Our Presidential Nominees*, edited by William G. Mayer, 105–57. Chatham, NJ: Chatham House, 1996.

———. "Forecasting Nominations." In *In Pursuit of the White House: How We Choose Our Presidential Nominees*, edited by William G. Mayer, 44–71. Chatham, NJ: Chatham House, 1996.

———. "The Presidential Nominations." In *The Election of 2000*, edited by Gerald M. Pomper, 12–45. New York: Chatham House, 2001.

———. "What the Founders Intended: Another Look at the Origins of the American Presidential Selection Process." In *The Making of the Presidential Candidates 2008*, edited by William G. Mayer, 203–34. Lanham, MD: Rowman & Littlefield, 2008.

———. "Superdelegates: Reforming the Reforms Revisited." In *Reforming the Presidential Nomination Process*, edited by Steven S. Smith and Melanie J. Springer, 85–108. Washington, DC: Brookings Institution, 2009.

Mayer, William G., and Andrew E. Busch. "Can the Federal Government Reform the Presidential Nomination Process?" *Election Law Journal* 3 (2004): 613–25.

———. *The Front-Loading Problem in Presidential Nominations*. Washington, DC: Brookings Institution, 2004.

McCann, James A. "The Emerging International Trend toward Open Presidential Primaries: The American Presidential Nomination Process in Comparative Perspective." In *The Making of the Presidential Candidates 2004*, edited by William G. Mayer, 265–93. Lanham, MD: Rowman & Littlefield, 2004.

McDonald, Michael. United States Election Project, 2008 General Election Turnout Rates. Available at http://elections.gmu.edu/Turnout_2008G.html (accessed July 8, 2009).

Moran, Jack, and Mark Fenster. "Voter Turnout in Presidential Primaries: A Diachronic Analysis." *American Politics Quarterly* 10 (1982): 453–76.

Murphy, Cullen. "Primary Considerations." *Atlantic Monthly*, April 2004.

Murray, Shailagh, and Paul Kane. "In Background, a Battle for Superdelegates: Clinton Ahead Among Party Leaders, but Threat of a Wholesale Shift Remains." *Washington Post*, January 30, 2008.

National Association of Secretaries of State, *The Case for Regional Presidential Primaries in 2012 and Beyond*, February 2008. Available at http://nass.org/index.php?option=com_content&task=view&id=74&Itemid=210 (accessed November 19, 2009).

Newport, Frank. "Obama Gains among Former Clinton Supporters." *Gallup Poll*, September 2, 2008.

Norrander, Barbara. "Explaining Cross-State Variation in Independents." *American Journal of Political Science* 33 (1989): 516–36.

———. "Ideological Representativeness of Presidential Primary Voters." *American Journal of Political Science* 33 (1989): 570–87.

———. *Super Tuesday: Regional Politics and Presidential Primaries*. Lexington: University Press of Kentucky, 1992.

———. "Nomination Choices: Caucus and Primary Outcomes, 1976–1988." *American Journal of Political Science* 37 (1993): 343–64.

———. "Field Essay: Presidential Nomination Politics in the Post-Reform Era." *Political Research Quarterly* 49 (1996): 875–915.

———. "The Attrition Game: Initial Resources, Initial Contests and the Exit of Candidates During the US Presidential Primary Season." *British Journal of Political Science* 36 (2006): 487–507.

———. "Democratic Marathon, Republican Sprint." In *The American Elections of 2008*, edited by Janet M. Box-Steffensmeier and Steven E. Schier, 33–54. Lanham, MD: Rowman & Littlefield, 2009.

———. "Public Support for Presidential Nomination Reform." *Public Opinion Quarterly* 73 (2009): 578–89.

———. "Lessons from the 1988 Southern Regional Primary." In *The Rise of the West in Presidential Elections*. Salt Lake City: University of Utah Press, forthcoming.

Overacker, Louise. *The Presidential Primary*. New York: Macmillan, 1926.

Paolino, Phillip, and Daron R. Shaw. "Lifting the Hood on the Straight-Talk Express: Examining the McCain Phenomenon." *American Politics Research* 29 (2001): 483–506.

Parmelee, John. "Presidential Primary Videocassettes: How Candidates in the 2000 U.S. Presidential Primary Elections Framed Their Early Campaigns." *Political Communication* 19 (2002): 317–31.

Patterson, Thomas E. *The Mass Media Election: How Americans Choose Their President*. New York: Praeger, 1980.

Polsby, Nelson W. *Consequences of Party Reform*. New York: Oxford University Press, 1983.

Pomper, Gerald M. *Nominating the President: The Politics of Convention Choice*. Evanston, IL: Northwestern University Press, 1966.

———. "The Nominating Contests and Conventions." In *The Election of 1976: Reports and Interpretations*, edited by Gerald Pomper, 1–34. New York: David McKay, 1977.

———. "New Rules and New Games in Presidential Nominations." *Journal of Politics* 41 (1979): 784–805.

"Primary Train Wreck." *Boston Globe*, January 17, 2008.

Project for Excellence in Journalism and the Joan Shorenstein Center on Press, Politics and Public Policy at Harvard University. "The Invisible Primary—Invisible No Longer." Available at http://www.journalism.org/node/8187 (accessed December 17, 2009).

———. "McCain Wins the Coverage Battle as Media Move to Anoint Him." Available at http://www.journalism.org/node/9610 (accessed December 17, 2009).

———. "Post-Pennsylvania Spin Drowns Out McCain." Available at http://www.journalism.org/node/10824 (accessed December 17, 2009).

Ranney, Austin. "Changing the Rules of the Nominating Game." In *Choosing the President*, edited by James David Barber, 71–94. Englewood Cliffs, NJ: Prentice-Hall, 1974.

———. *Curing the Mischief of Faction: Party Reform in America*. Berkeley: University of California Press, 1975.

———. *Participation in American Presidential Nominations, 1976*. Washington, DC: American Enterprise Institute, 1977.

Ray, P. Orman. "Reform of Presidential Nominating Methods." *Annals of the American Academy of Political and Social Science* 106 (1923): 63–71.

Reiter, Howard L. *Selecting the President: The Nominating Process in Transition.* Philadelphia: University of Pennsylvania Press, 1985.

Republican National Committee. *Nominating Future Presidents.* Washington, DC: Republican National Committee, 2000.

———. *Call for the 2008 Republican National Convention.* Washington, DC: Republican National Committee, 2007.

Riker, William H. *Liberalism Against Populism.* San Francisco: W. H. Freeman, 1982.

Robinson, Michael J., and Margaret A. Sheehan. *Over the Wire and on TV.* New York: Russell Sage Foundation, 1983.

Roche, John P. "The Founding Fathers: A Reform Caucus in Action." *American Political Science Review* 55 (1961): 799–816.

Rothenberg, Lawrence S., and Richard A. Brody. "Participation in Presidential Primaries." *Western Political Quarterly* 41 (1988): 253–71.

Rubins, Richard L. "Presidential Primaries: Continuities, Dimensions of Change, and Political Implications." In *The Party Symbol: Readings on Political Parties,* edited by William Crotty, 126–47. San Francisco: W. H. Freeman, 1980.

Sabato, Larry J. "Picking Presidential Nominees: Time for a New Regime." In *Reforming the Presidential Nomination Process,* edited by Steven S. Smith and Melanie J. Springer, 136–50. Washington, DC: Brookings Institution, 2009.

Sautter, R. Craig, and Edward M. Burke. *Inside the Wigwam: Chicago Presidential Conventions 1860–1996.* Chicago: Wild Onion Books, 1996.

Scott, Jeffry. "Countdown 2008: Road to the White House; McKinney Gets Green Party Nomination for Presidency; Ex-House Rep from DeKalb on Most Ballots." *Atlanta Journal-Constitution,* July 13, 2008.

Shafer, Byron, and Amber Wichowsky. "Institutional Structure and Democratic Values: A Research Note on a Natural Experiment." *The Forum,* Volume 7, Issue 2, Article 2 (2009), http://www.bepress.com/forum/vol7/iss2/art2 (accessed March 5, 2010).

Sheinin, Aaron Gould. "Libertarians Pick Barr as Nominee." *Atlanta Journal-Constitution,* May 26, 2008.

Sorauf, Frank J. *Party Politics in America,* 3rd edition. Boston: Little, Brown, 1976.

Southwell, Priscilla L. "The 1984 Democratic Nomination Process: The Significance of Unpledged Superdelegates." *American Politics Quarterly* 14 (1986): 75–88.

Squire, Peverill. "Iowa and the Nomination Process." In *The Iowa Caucuses and the Presidential Nominating Process,* edited by Peverill Squire, 1–19. Boulder, CO: Westview Press, 1989.

Steger, Wayne P. "Presidential Renomination Challenges in the 20th Century." *Presidential Studies Quarterly* 33 (2003): 827–52.

———. "How Did the Primary Vote Forecasts Fare in 2008?" *Presidential Studies Quarterly* 39 (2009): 141–54.

Steger, Wayne P., Andrew J. Dowdle, and Randall E. Adkins. "The New Hampshire Effect in Presidential Nominations." *Political Research Quarterly* 57 (2004): 375–90.

———. "Seeking Competitive Advantage: How Presidential Candidates and Party Networks Adapt to Times of Social, Economic, and Technological Change."

Paper presented at the State of the Parties Conference, Ray Bliss Institute, University of Akron, October 15–16, 2009.

Stone, Walter J., Lonna Rae Atkeson, and Ronald B. Rapoport. "Turning On or Turning Off?: Mobilization and Demobilization Effects of Participation in Presidential Nomination Campaigns." *American Journal of Political Science* 36 (1992): 665–91.

Stone, Walter J., Ronald B. Rapoport, and Alan I. Abramowitz. "Candidate Support in Presidential Nomination Campaigns: The Case of Iowa in 1984." *Journal of Politics* 54 (1992): 1074–97.

Sundquist, James L. "The Crisis of Competence in Our National Government." *Political Science Quarterly* 95 (1980): 183–208.

"Super, But Still Flawed: Early Vote Worked for California, but ..." *Sacramento Bee*, February 7, 2008.

Vargas, Jose Antonio. "Campaign.USA: With the Internet Comes a New Political 'Clickocracy'." *Washington Post*, April 1, 2008.

Von Sternberg, Bob, and Steve Brandt. "Ballot Count By Hand Starts in Minneapolis." *Star Tribune*, November 4, 2009.

Watson, Richard A. *The Presidential Contest.* New York: Wiley, 1980.

White, Theodore H. *The Making of the President 1960.* New York: Atheneum House, 1961.

———. *The Making of the President 1964.* New York: Atheneum, 1965.

———. *The Making of the President 1968.* New York: Atheneum, 1969.

Wilcox, Clyde. "Internet Fundraising in 2008: A New Model?" *The Forum*, Volume 6, Issue 1, Article 6 (2008), http://www.bepress.com/forum/vol6/iss1/art6 (accessed March 5, 2010).

Will, George F. "Messy, But Not a Mess." *Newsweek*, November 5, 2007.

Williams, Christine B., and Girish "Jeff" Gulati. "What is a Social Network Worth?: Facebook and Vote Share in the 2008 Presidential Primaries." Paper presented at the annual meeting of the American Political Science Association, Boston, MA, August 28–31, 2008.

Wilson, James Q. *The Amateur Democrat: Club Politics in Three Cities.* Chicago: University of Chicago Press, 1962.

Wilson, Woodrow. First Annual Message to Congress, December 2, 1913. Available at the Miller Center of Public Affairs, University of Virginia, http://miller-center.org/scripps/archive/speeches/detail/3789 (accessed November 23, 2009).

Witcover, Jules. "The McCain Dilemma." *Salt Lake City Tribune*, July 13, 2007.

Court Cases

Buckley v. Valeo, 424 U.S. 1 (1976).

California Democratic Party v. Jones, 530 U.S. 567 (2000).

Cousins v. Wigoda, 419 U.S. 477 (1974).

Davis v. Federal Election Commission, 501 F. Supp. 2d 22 (2008).

Democratic Party v. Wisconsin ex rel. La Follette, 450 U.S. 107 (1981).

Tashjian v. Republican Party of Connecticut, 479 U.S. 208 (1986).

Index

Note: Page numbers followed by 'f' refer to figures, followed by 'n' refer to notes, and followed by 't' refer to tables.